OUR CONSTITUTION

and What It Means

SIXTH, BICENTENNIAL EDITION

Simplified and Explained by

WILLIAM KOTTMEYER
Author-in-Residence, School Division
and
Former Superintendent of Schools,
St. Louis, Missouri

THOMAS F. EAGLETON
Former U.S. Senator from Missouri
and
University Professor of Public Affairs,
Washington University, St. Louis, Missouri

SCHOOL DIVISION/McGRAW-HILL BOOK COMPANY
New York   St. Louis   San Francisco   Dallas   Oklahoma City   Atlanta

Executive Editor: Alma Graham
Editing and Styling/Formatting: Linda Richmond
Design Supervision/Electronic Page Makeup: Valerie Greco
Photo Editing Manager: Suzanne V. Skloot
Senior Production Supervisor: Judith Tisdale

Art Editor: Ann Craig
Photo Editor: Nancy E. Grimes
Research Assistant to Former Senator Eagleton: Michael Reis
Artists: Steve Petruccio and Barbara Steadman, represented by Evelyn Johnson, Assoc.
Cover Design: Levavi & Levavi

Library of Congress Cataloging-in-Publication Data
United States.
 Our Constitution and what it means.

 Summary: Presents the Constitution of the United States and includes a simple explanation of
its contents.
 1. United States—Constitutional law—Juvenile literature. [1. United States—Constitutional law]
I. Kottmeyer, William, date. II. Eagleton, Thomas F., date. III. Title.
KF4550.Z9U55 1987 342.73'023 86-21436
ISBN 0-07-034840-5 347.30223

Photo Credits
8: The Granger Collection; **9:** NYPL/Life Magazine; **11:** (tr) John Lewis Stage/The Image Bank,
(mr, bl) Library of Congress, (br) Culver Pictures; **12:** (tl) The Granger Collection, (m) Ralph Earl/
Yale University Art Gallery; **14:** (ml, br) Culver Pictures; **15:** Howard C. Christy/Architect of Capitol;
16: (t) New York Historical Society; **17:** (t) J. L. Atlan/Sygma, (b) Jim Pickerell/Click/Chicago;
18: The Granger Collection; **19:** (t) John Ficara/Woodfin Camp & Assoc., (b) Historical Picture
Service; **20:** C. L. Chryslin/The Image Bank; **42:** (tl) FDR Memorial Library, (tr) H. J. Keller/Vermont
Division of Historic Preservation, (bl) George Silk/Life Magazine, (br) Cecil Stoughton/The White House;
53: Monkmeyer Press; **63:** Culver Pictures; **70:** (t) The Bettmann Archive, (b) FDR Memorial Library;
74: (tl) David Harris/Princeton University, Firestone Library, (bl) The White House; **75:** G. Cloyd/
Taurus Photos; **77:** (bl, tr) Peter Vadnai/McGraw-Hill; **78:** (tl) Frank Johnston/Black Star, (tr) William
Hubbell/Woodfin Camp & Assoc., (bl) Billy E. Barnes, (bm) Larry Voight/Photo Researchers, (br) Scott
Thode/International Stock Photo; **79:** (tr) Christopher Springmann/The Stock Market, (tl) Leonard Freed/
Magnum, (b) G. E. Pakenham/International Stock Photo; **80:** (bl) Blair Seitz/Photo Researchers, (tr) Billy
E. Barnes/Southern Light, (tl) M. Nelson/FPG International, (br) Robert Capece/McGraw-Hill, (tm) Eve
Arnold/Magnum; **81:** (tl) Bill Stanton/International Stock Photo, (tr) Jim Erickson/The Stock Market,
(bl) Scott Thode/International Stock Photo, (br) Butch Martin/The Image Bank; **82:** (b) Mimi Forsyth/
Monkmeyer Press, (tr) George Ancona/International Stock Photo, (tl) Mickey Pfleger; **83:** (bl) The
Stock Market, (tl) René Burri/Magnum, (tm) Constantine Manos/Magnum, (br) Kay Chernush/The Image
Bank, (tr) Dale Winter/The Image Bank; **84:** (bl) Nick Pavloff/The Image Bank, (tl) Michael Ventura/
Bruce Coleman, (tr) Billy E. Barnes/Southern Light, (mr) John Lewis Stage/The Image Bank, (br) Magnum

1 2 3 4 5 6 7 8 9 10 WEBWEB 95 94 93 92 91 90 89 88 87 86

TABLE OF CONTENTS

Correlated Material:
Test for OUR CONSTITUTION   Sixth, Bicentennial Edition

FOREWORD

Prompted by the Missouri Legislature's enactment of a law requiring students of the state's elementary, secondary, and college institutions to pass a test on the United States Constitution in order to graduate, Dr. William Kottmeyer, in 1949, wrote a simplified version of the Constitution in essentially the same three-column format of this sixth and bicentennial edition. He did so because, as he then stated in a teacher's foreword, a substantial number of junior and senior high school students did not have sufficient skill to read and understand the original version.

Dr. Kottmeyer's document, first done for the St. Louis Public Schools, was subsequently published and was widely sold by the Webster Publishing Company, now part of the School Division of McGraw-Hill Book Company. For more than three decades, it has been used in every state of the nation.

The coauthor of this enlarged and updated sixth edition of *Our Constitution and What It Means* is former United States Senator Thomas F. Eagleton of Missouri, who brings to this new publication an extraordinary background of practical experience in dealing with modern constitutional issues and who has earned widespread respect both as a writer and as a much-respected constitutional commentator.

Mr. Eagleton served as a public official for 30 years: as Circuit Attorney for the City of St. Louis, Attorney General of Missouri, Lt. Governor of Missouri, and U.S. Senator from Missouri, a post he held for 18 years. While serving in the Senate, Mr. Eagleton wrote *War and Presidential Power,* a chronicle of the enactment of the War Powers Resolution. He currently serves on the faculty of Washington University in St. Louis as a University Professor of Public Affairs.

This new edition, like its predecessors, is intended to lighten the burden of instructors who have the responsibility of familiarizing youngsters or adults of widely varying reading ability with the basic ideas of our Constitution. After a short and simple account of the writing of the Constitution, the material is presented in three columns. The middle column reprints the original form of the Constitution, with the capitalization and the punctuation brought up to date. The right-hand column—"What It Means"—is a parallel rewrite of the original in the simplest possible form, about the fifth grade level of reading difficulty. The left-hand column—"Some Things to Know"—helps readers understand more fully what they are reading. It provides historical background and interprets specific words and phrases in the Constitution. Discussion questions are included after each major section of the Constitution. In closing, there is a consideration of "What the Constitution Means to You"—a summary of some of the rights and privileges the Constitution gives to all Americans.

The "Constitution Vocabulary" at the end gives simple explanations of words and terms with which many readers may not be familiar. A "Presidents and Vice Presidents Chart" is also included, giving each President's political party, term of office, and Vice President. A separate multiple-choice test covering the Constitution contains 100 items and is provided to save busy instructors' time. An Answer Key accompanies the test.

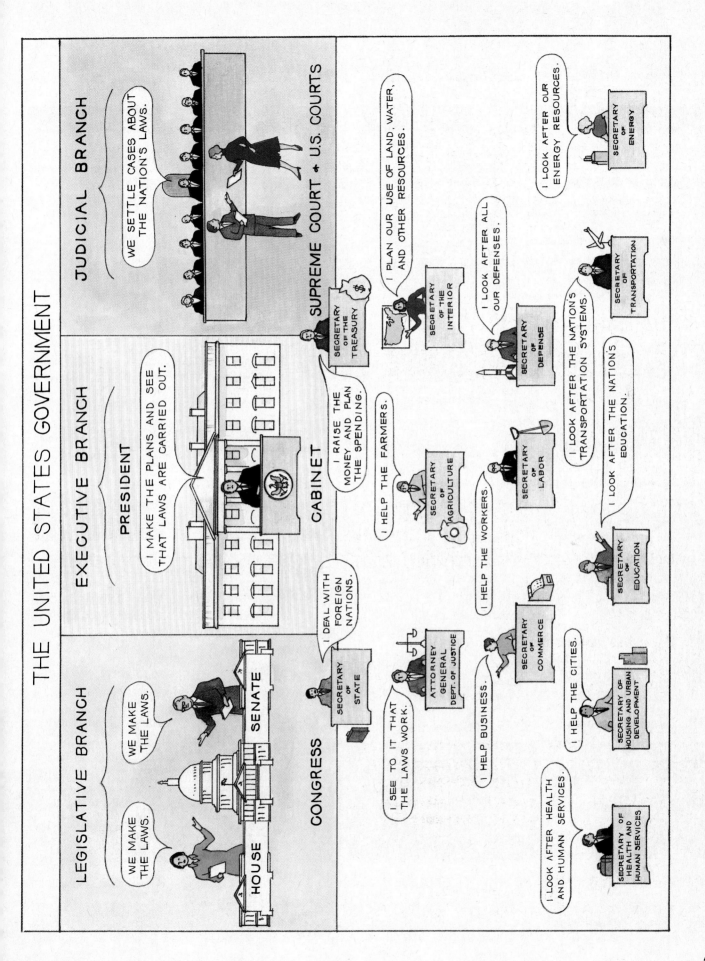

5

PRESIDENTS AND VICE PRESIDENTS CHART

Name	Political Party	Term	Vice President
1. George Washington	Federalist	1789–1797 2 terms	John Adams
2. John Adams	Federalist	1797–1801 1 term	Thomas Jefferson
3. Thomas Jefferson	Democratic-Republican	1801–1809 2 terms	Aaron Burr George Clinton
4. James Madison	Democratic-Republican	1809–1817 2 terms	George Clinton Elbridge Gerry
5. James Monroe	Democratic-Republican	1817–1825 2 terms	Daniel D. Tompkins
6. John Quincy Adams	Democratic-Republican	1825–1829 1 term	John C. Calhoun
7. Andrew Jackson	Democratic	1829–1837 2 terms	John C. Calhoun Martin Van Buren
8. Martin Van Buren	Democratic	1837–1841 1 term	Richard M. Johnson
9. William Henry Harrison	Whig	1841 1 mo	John Tyler
10. John Tyler	Whig	1841–1845 3 yr, 11 mo	No Vice President
11. James K. Polk	Democratic	1845–1849 1 term	George M. Dallas
12. Zachary Taylor	Whig	1849–1850 1 yr, 4 mo	Millard Fillmore
13. Millard Fillmore	Whig	1850–1853 2 yr, 8 mo	No Vice President
14. Franklin Pierce	Democratic	1853–1857 1 term	William Rufus de Vane King
15. James Buchanan	Democratic	1857–1861 1 term	John C. Breckinridge
16. Abraham Lincoln	Republican	1861–1865 1 term, 1 mo, 10 days	Hannibal Hamlin Andrew Johnson
17. Andrew Johnson	National Union	1865–1869 3 yr, 10 mo, 20 days	No Vice President
18. Ulysses S. Grant	Republican	1869–1877 2 terms	Schuyler Colfax Henry Wilson
19. Rutherford B. Hayes	Republican	1877–1881 1 term	William A. Wheeler
20. James A. Garfield	Republican	1881 6 mo, 15 days	Chester A. Arthur

Name	Political Party	Term	Vice President
21. Chester A. Arthur	Republican	1881–1885 3 yr, 5 mo, 15 days	No Vice President
22. Grover Cleveland	Democratic	1885–1889 1 term	Thomas A. Hendricks
23. Benjamin Harrison	Republican	1889–1893 1 term	Levi P. Morton
24. Grover Cleveland	Democratic	1893–1897 1 term	Adlai E. Stevenson
25. William McKinley	Republican	1897–1901 1 term, 6 mo, 10 days	Garret A. Hobart Theodore Roosevelt
26. Theodore Roosevelt	Republican	1901–1909 1 term, 3 yr, 5 mo	Charles W. Fairbanks
27. William H. Taft	Republican	1909–1913 1 term	James S. Sherman
28. Woodrow Wilson	Democratic	1913–1921 2 terms	Thomas R. Marshall
29. Warren G. Harding	Republican	1921–1923 2 yr, 5 mo	Calvin Coolidge
30. Calvin Coolidge	Republican	1923–1929 1 term, 1 yr, 7 mo	Charles G. Dawes
31. Herbert C. Hoover	Republican	1929–1933 1 term	Charles Curtis
32. Franklin D. Roosevelt	Democratic	1933–1945 3 terms, 3 mo	John N. Garner, Henry A. Wallace, Harry S Truman
33. Harry S Truman	Democratic	1945–1953 1 term, 3 yr, 9 mo	Alben W. Barkley
34. Dwight D. Eisenhower	Republican	1953–1961 2 terms	Richard M. Nixon
35. John F. Kennedy	Democratic	1961–1963 2 yr, 10 mo	Lyndon B. Johnson
36. Lyndon B. Johnson	Democratic	1963–1969 1 term, 1 yr, 2 mo	Hubert H. Humphrey
37. Richard M. Nixon	Republican	1969–1974 1 term, 1 yr, 6 mo, 20 days	Spiro T. Agnew Gerald R. Ford
38. Gerald R. Ford	Republican	1974–1977 2 yr, 5 mo, 11 days	Nelson A. Rockefeller
39. James E. Carter, Jr.	Democratic	1977–1981 1 term	Walter F. Mondale
40. Ronald W. Reagan	Republican	1981–	George H. W. Bush

THE STORY OF OUR CONSTITUTION

In the 1600s, America was settled by the English and ruled by England. In 1707, England united with Scotland to form Great Britain. By the year 1774, our 13 British colonies had had enough of the rule of British kings. That year 12 colonies sent delegates to Philadelphia to talk things over. These representatives became our Continental Congress. Soon all 13 colonies had representatives in Congress.

Congress met again in 1776. The members agreed to fight in order to be free of Great Britain. They adopted Thomas Jefferson's beautifully written Declaration of Independence. That famous piece of writing states the rights of free people.

George Washington then led American soldiers to victory in the Revolutionary War. The 13 colonies became the 13 United States of America.

(Opposite) On July 3, 1776, while 35,000 British soldiers prepared to land in New York, these men were discussing the Declaration of Independence. From left to right, they are Benjamin Franklin, Thomas Jefferson, Robert Livingston, John Adams, and Roger Sherman.

(Below) On December 25, 1776, Washington and his revolutionary army crossed the Delaware River. They surprised the enemy on the other side the next day and won a battle in Trenton, New Jersey.

THE ARTICLES OF CONFEDERATION

While the war went on, the Continental Congress had to form a government. The members of this Congress wrote a set of rules. They called them the Articles of Confederation. This was our first constitution.

The Articles of Confederation were very weak. The people did not want a strong central government. They had had one under British rule. Each state wanted to be its own boss.

The Articles of Confederation called for a congress, but they let the states keep their power. Each state got one vote. There was no President. There were state courts, but there was no Supreme Court. Congress could pass laws, but the states did not have to obey them.

Congress needed money during the war. Later money was needed to pay the war debts. But Congress had no power to tax people. Nobody would lend Congress money. Congress had no way to pay it back. Congress could and did ask the states for money. Often the states refused to give.

Congress had other money problems. It had no gold or silver, so it could not mint coins. It could print paper money, but nobody would take it. The people used what they had—British and Spanish coins and paper money printed by the states.

Congress had no power to tax goods going to or coming from other lands. The states often did tax goods coming from other states. People often quarreled about these state taxes.

Congress tried to make treaties with other nations. But any state could break any treaty. Congress could do nothing about it.

Congress could ask for an army, but it could not make men serve as soldiers. Congress had no money to pay soldiers.

The states were more powerful than Congress.

Congress had no money to pay its soldiers. The states could ignore Congress's laws and treaties.

The members of Congress knew they must have more power. Three times they asked that the Articles of Confederation be changed. Each time one or two states turned them down. All states had to agree to changes before Congress could make any.

Leaders from five states met again in Annapolis in 1786. There they proposed that the states send representatives to Philadelphia to revise the Articles of Confederation. Congress agreed. And so the meeting of the Constitutional Convention began on May 25, 1787.

Twelve states answered the call. Rhode Island did not send anybody. That state wanted no part of a strong national government. But 55 representatives from 12 states did show up. They came to Philadelphia and met in Independence Hall.

FAMOUS AMERICANS HELP

Virginia sent its Revolutionary War hero, George Washington. The others elected Washington to preside over the meeting.

Virginia also sent James Madison, who was 36 years old. He came to every meeting. He kept notes and spoke 161 times! He became known as the "Father of the Constitution."

Clever George Mason was another important representative from Virginia. He was worried about a strong central government. He thought the old Articles of Confederation could be patched up.

Pennsylvania sent 81-year-old Benjamin Franklin. Wise old Ben helped keep the peace at the convention when the debates grew hot.

From Pennsylvania, too, came Robert Morris. It was he who had raised money to buy guns for Washington's troops.

And from that state also came Gouverneur Morris. He was later given the job of writing the final Constitution in clear English.

The stirring words of the Declaration of Independence were first heard in this room in Independence Hall, Philadelphia.

John Hancock, with his hand outstretched, announces to the crowd that the Declaration has been signed.

James Madison proposed the amendments in the Bill of Rights.

During the war, Robert Morris took charge of America's finances.

Alexander Hamilton wrote 51 articles for newspapers to help win votes for the Constitution. His articles, along with others, appeared as *The Federalist*.

Roger Sherman helped guarantee the rights of small states.

From New York came the banker Alexander Hamilton. He had become General Washington's secretary during the war. He had helped get the Philadelphia meeting to take place.

Connecticut sent Roger Sherman. It was he who settled the differences between the big states and little states. He signed the Declaration of Independence and the Articles of Confederation as well as the Constitution.

These representatives had been sent to Philadelphia to make changes in the Articles of Confederation. After they talked things over, they decided to start from scratch. They would write a new Constitution for the new United States!

And that is what they did. By doing so they set up, or founded, our government. That is why we call them our Founding Fathers.

A THREE-PART GOVERNMENT

At that time, each state government had three parts: a governor, an assembly of lawmakers, and some courts and judges. It seemed sensible to form a three-branch government for the whole nation. The persons who would carry out, or execute, the laws became the *executive branch*. The people elected by the voters to make the laws became the *legislative branch*. The courts and the judges became the *judicial branch*.

The three branches of the federal government were modeled after the three-branch governments of the states.

The Executive Branch

Nobody wanted another king like George III. The Constitution writers wanted their chief executive, or President, to have power—but not too much power. They were afraid to let the common people elect him. The common people, they thought, might not have enough education or information to vote for good candidates. And so they had the people vote for electors. The electors would then elect a President. They called these electors the *Electoral College*.

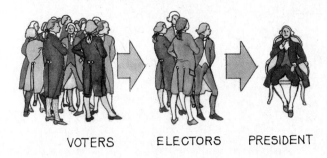

VOTERS   ELECTORS   PRESIDENT

The electoral system

The Legislative Branch

The Articles of Confederation gave each state one vote in the Congress. Big states like New York did not like that idea. They said if you had more people, you ought to have more votes. The little states like Delaware wanted as many votes as the big states had.

The arguments often got heated. Some of the representatives got angry and went home. But the way to stop a fight is simple. You have both sides give in a little. When they do, they make a compromise. But how could the big and little states compromise?

States with many people thought they should have more votes in Congress than states with fewer people.

At last Roger Sherman of Connecticut came up with a clever idea. "Let's have two houses in our legislative branch," he said. "We'll call one branch the *House of Representatives*. The other will be the *Senate*. In the House, the number of votes will depend on the number of people in the state. In the Senate, each state will have two votes." Roger Sherman's compromise made sense. The other Constitution writers agreed to follow his suggestion.

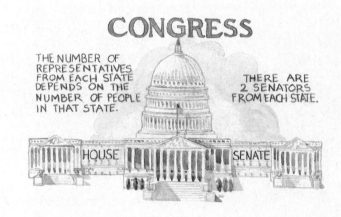

CONGRESS

THE NUMBER OF REPRESENTATIVES FROM EACH STATE DEPENDS ON THE NUMBER OF PEOPLE IN THAT STATE.

THERE ARE 2 SENATORS FROM EACH STATE.

HOUSE   SENATE

But there was still a problem. How were slaves to be counted in figuring out the population of each state? Because most slaves were in the South, the Southern states wanted to count each slave as one person. If they did, the South would be entitled to a larger number of votes in the House of Representatives. The Northern states did not like this plan. In fact, many people in the North wanted to stop the slave trade. The fight ended in another compromise. Each slave would be counted as three-fifths of a person. The North agreed that Congress would leave the slave trade alone until 1808.

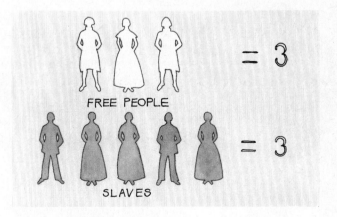

FREE PEOPLE = 3

SLAVES = 3

Each slave counted as 3/5 of a person for taxation and representation purposes.

13

The Supreme Court was created as the highest court in the United States.

Gouverneur Morris wrote the final Constitution in a way that made it clear and precise.

Mercy Otis Warren

Abigail Adams

The Judicial Branch

The members did not spend much time debating the judicial branch. They agreed to have a *Supreme Court*. It would be the highest court in the land. It would decide whether federal, state, and local courts had acted in line with the Constitution.

SIGNING THE CONSTITUTION

It was near the end of the Convention. George Mason of Virginia and Elbridge Gerry of Massachusetts still wanted a bill of rights. But it was getting late. It was hot. Everybody wanted to go home. The debates ended without adding a bill of rights to the Constitution. The members wanted somebody to put the new Constitution into clear language. Gouverneur Morris was a highly respected writer. He wrote it all in 4,300 words and delivered it 2 days later.

On September 17, 1787, 39 of the 55 representatives signed the new Constitution. They represented 12 states. You can see what happened in artist Howard Chandler Christy's picture on page 15. It hangs in our Capitol in Washington, DC.

RATIFYING THE CONSTITUTION

The cries for a bill of rights grew louder while the representatives were ratifying the Constitution. Elbridge Gerry, George Mason, and Patrick Henry spoke against accepting the Constitution because it had no guarantee of a person's rights. Mercy Otis Warren also spoke out strongly against it. She wanted a bill of rights—and a better deal for women.

The friends of the Constitution worked equally hard to get it passed. They made speeches and wrote articles and letters to the newspapers. Led by Alexander Hamilton, James Madison, and John Jay, they were known as the Federalists. They wrote 85 letters to the newspapers to win New York votes.

Mercy Otis Warren's anti-British play, *The Blockheads*, was published in Boston and Philadelphia with the help of John Adams. (Detail of *Mercy Otis Warren* by John S. Copley, Museum of Fine Arts, Boston)

Abigail Adams wrote a letter to her husband while he was at the constitutional convention. In it, she wrote ". . . we [women] will not hold ourselves bound by any Laws in which we have no voice."

The signing of the Constitution took place on September 17, 1787.

1. George Washington
2. Benjamin Franklin
3. James Madison, Jr.
4. Alexander Hamilton
5. Gouverneur Morris
6. Robert Morris
7. James Wilson
8. Charlers C. Pinckney
9. Charles Pinckney
10. John Rutledge

11. Pierce Butler
12. Roger Sherman
13. William S. Johnson
14. James McHenry
15. George Read
16. Richard Bassett
17. Richard D. Spaight
18. William Blount
19. Hugh Williamson
20. Dan of St. Thomas Jenifer

21. Rufus King
22. Nathaniel Gorham
23. Jonathan Dayton
24. Daniel Carroll
25. William Few
26. Abraham Baldwin
27. John Langdon
28. Nicholas Gilman
29. William Livingston
30. William Paterson

31. Thomas Mifflin
32. George Clymer
33. Thomas FitzSimons
34. Jared Ingersoll
35. Gunning Bedford, Jr.
36. Jacob Broom
37. John Dickinson
38. John Blair
39. David Brearley
40. William Jackson

15

In 1789, Washington became the first President of the United States. He was sworn in in New York City, the nation's first capital.

The First Amendment guarantees freedom of religion.

Nine states had to accept the Constitution to make it the law of the land. New Hampshire was the ninth state to ratify it. Thus on June 21, 1788, the Constitution went into effect.

The states then chose their presidential electors. On February 4, 1789, these electors chose George Washington as the first President of the United States.

But North Carolina and Rhode Island still refused to ratify. They did agree to join the others if Congress would add a bill of rights to the Constitution. Several other states said they would ratify the Constitution only if such a bill of rights were added. Madison saw what had to be done. He promised to have Congress add the bill of rights after the states had accepted the Constitution.

True to his word, he proposed 12 amendments. Congress passed them. By December 15, 1791, 11 states had accepted 10 of the amendments. Thus, they became a part of the Constitution. We call these first 10 amendments the *Bill of Rights*.

THE BILL OF RIGHTS

Having a bill of rights added to the Constitution made sense. Most state constitutions already had clear statements about the rights of the people. In fact, many Americans felt that a good constitution must have such statements. Thomas Jefferson wrote, "A bill of rights is what the people are entitled to against every government on earth." Jefferson wanted to delay accepting the Constitution until a bill of rights was added. There was not much agreement about what should be said in a bill of rights. Seventy-eight different proposals were sent into Congress.

You can see from the following examples why people wanted a bill of rights so badly.

The First Amendment

The first amendment says that Congress may not make laws that set up a religion. In other words, the federal government may not back or favor anybody's religion. The Constitution writers knew that many governments had done that. The amendment also says that Congress may make no law to stop you from following your religion. This means government may not interfere with the way you worship.

The government may not keep you from saying or writing what you think, either. It also may not punish you after you stand up for your rights. Of course, there are some limits to free speech. You have no right to tell lies about a person. You have no right to threaten public safety by yelling "Fire!" as a joke in a crowded theater.

If people are going to have a free country, the newspapers must be free to say what they want to. They should be free to say what is wrong with the government. The First Amendment gives the newspapers these rights. Newspapers should not print things that will put the country in danger, though.

The Fourth Amendment

This amendment protects you and your property. The colonists had been angry when British soldiers barged into their homes for any reason at all. The Constitution writers wanted us to feel safe in our own homes. And so the police, for example, may not burst into your home when they feel like it. They must first prove to a judge that they have a good reason to search your home. If they can do so, the judge may give them a warrant to search. You have a right to see the warrant before you let them in.

Steelworkers peacefully speak out for their rights near the White House.

The Fifth Amendment

The Fifth Amendment protects your rights when you are accused of a crime. It says that people do not have to go to court for a crime that would mean death or jail unless a grand jury has accused them. (A grand jury is a group of people chosen to decide whether there is enough evidence to hold a trial.) For serious crimes, you have the right to a trial by a jury. You do not have to say anything against yourself in court. In fact, police have to warn suspects that they have the right to a lawyer and that they may remain silent. It is up to your accuser to prove you are guilty. You cannot be tried twice for the same crime. The Fifth Amendment tries to make sure that the law will treat everyone fairly.

OTHER IMPORTANT AMENDMENTS

You can see that our Constitution writers were wise to provide a way to add amendments to the Constitution. It is amazing that the Bill of Rights, written so many years ago, works so well for us today. The first 10 amendments give all of us freedom and fair treatment. Although the first 10

All citizens are guaranteed a fair and public trial by jury.

Lincoln (left) read the Emancipation Proclamation to his Cabinet first. In the months that followed, thousands of Blacks joined the Union army to fight for freedom.

After the Civil War, in 1867, Blacks voted for the first time in Iowa and Dakota.

amendments did much to protect our rights, we have added 16 other amendments, too. There are now 26 amendments to the Constitution. Among the most important are the Thirteenth, Fourteenth, Fifteenth, and Nineteenth amendments.

The Thirteenth Amendment

The Thirteenth Amendment, which was passed in 1865, plainly and flatly ended slavery. During the Constitutional Convention, leaders like Washington, Jefferson, Madison, and Mason were against slavery. They knew it was evil, even though they still owned slaves themselves. But they also knew the Southern states would never ratify the Constitution if it abolished slavery. So they put off the slavery question in order to get the Constitution passed.

The number of slaves grew fast. In 1790, there were about 700,000. When Lincoln was elected in 1860, there were 4 million. All Lincoln tried to do at that time was to keep slavery from spreading. As people moved westward across the Mississippi, more free states joined the Union. In 1861, fearing that Lincoln would end their slave system, 11 Southern states left the Union. They formed the Confederate States of America. The Civil War started.

Lincoln then declared the slaves in the Confederate states free. While the war went on, the border states kept their slaves. After the war ended, in 1865, the Thirteenth Amendment completed the wiping out of slavery in the United States.

The Fourteenth Amendment

The Fourteenth Amendment, adopted in 1868, was also very important. At that time, Blacks were still being treated as slaves in some places. The Fourteenth Amendment said that no state could enforce a law that kept United States citizens from getting their rights. It said that no state could take away a person's life, liberty, or property without fair treatment from the law. The words "due process of law" have come to mean that most of the Bill of Rights must be followed not only by the national government but by state governments as well. That means that anybody under United States rule is treated as fairly as anybody else. The amendment gives equal protection under the laws.

But from 1868 to 1954, the Supreme Court ruled that Blacks could be kept separate and still be treated equally. That meant you could have separate schools, eating places, and housing for Blacks and Whites. It meant you could have separate seats on buses. During those years, the separation of Blacks and Whites was constitutional.

But then the famous case *Brown vs. Board of Education of Topeka, Kansas,* came before the Supreme Court. The Supreme Court ruled in 1954 that "separate" schools were not "equal." The Constitution's promise of fair treatment for everybody finally came true for Black citizens.

The Fifteenth Amendment

The Fifteenth Amendment, passed in 1870, said that no state could keep a United States citizen from voting because of race. This gave Black men the right to vote.

The Nineteenth Amendment

The Nineteenth Amendment, passed in 1920, said that no state could keep a United States citizen from voting because she was a woman. This gave American women of all races the right to vote. In 1972, Congress voted for a proposed equal rights amendment (ERA) for women. However, only 35 of the needed 38 states ratified it within the time allowed. Thus, the amendment failed.

READING THE CONSTITUTION

That, in brief, is the story of our Constitution. The Constitution, itself, is not very long—only 4,300 words. It has an opening statement, or preamble. Then follow the seven articles and the amendments. Article I is about the legislative, or lawmaking, branch of government. Article II is about the executive branch. Article III is about our courts and judges—the judicial branch. Article IV tells what the U.S. government can do and what is left for the states to do. Article V gives ways for changing, or amending, the Constitution. Article VI deals with the nation's debt and the importance of the Constitution over state laws. Article VII gives the rules for putting the Constitution to work. The last part has the amendments.

Our Constitution became 200 years old in 1987. It has worked wonderfully well during those many years. No other nation's constitution has lasted so long. We Americans are proud of it. It is our guarantee of freedom. Here it is: the Constitution of the United States.

Integration is an example of change brought about by all branches of the government and by the efforts of individual people.

In 1869, the territory of Wyoming became the first place in the nation to give women the right to vote.

19

The Declaration of Independence, the Constitution, and the Bill of Rights are in the
National Archives in Washington, DC.

MEANING OF THE CONSTITUTION

Some Things to Know

The people had the Constitution written. No government forced it on them.

This means a "more perfect Union" than the one formed by the Articles of Confederation.

The Articles of Confederation did not give Congress the right to make people be soldiers.

Constitution of the U.S.

PREAMBLE

We, the people of the **United States, in order to form a more perfect Union, establish justice, insure domestic tranquility, provide for the common defense, promote the general welfare, and secure the blessings of liberty to ourselves and our posterity, do ordain and establish this Constitution for the United States of America.**

What It Means

INTRODUCTION

We Americans want to work together. We want everybody to be treated fairly. We want to get along with one another. We want to defend ourselves. We want things to run along smoothly. We want liberty for ourselves and our children. That is why we are writing this constitution for our nation.

SENATE + HOUSE OF REPRESENTATIVES = CONGRESS

The writers wanted the people they elected to make our laws.

They wanted *two* houses as a compromise between large and small states. The number of representatives depends on a state's population. Each state gets only two senators.

ARTICLE I

Section 1

All legislative powers herein granted shall be vested in a Congress of the United States, which shall consist of a Senate and House of Representatives.

ARTICLE I
LEGISLATIVE DEPARTMENT

Section 1
THE TWO HOUSES OF CONGRESS

Only Congress shall make laws for our entire nation. Congress shall have two houses: a House of Representatives and a Senate.

The Articles of Confederation called for a 1-year term. Representatives now have 2-year terms.

In the 1960s, the Supreme Court said that all House members must represent equal numbers of people.

There were many different ideas as to who should vote. The Constitution writers thought each state could better decide this itself.

In Great Britain, you can be a representative even if you do not live where the voters do.

Therefore, a woman could be and was elected before women were allowed to vote.

The Supreme Court said that Congress could not call for more taxes from big states just because they had more people. The Sixteenth Amendment solved the problem. This amendment gave Congress the right to collect income taxes, no matter how people earned the money or how many people there were in the state.

This means slaves. Slaves were not allowed to vote. When the states first paid taxes, they paid by the number of people they had. They counted three-fifths of their slaves. That made their taxes higher. The Southern states did not like that. But they got more representatives that way. The Thirteenth Amendment (1865) wiped out slavery. See also the Fourteenth and Fifteenth amendments.

Section 2

The House of Representatives shall be composed of members chosen every second year by the people of the several States, and the electors in each State shall have the qualifications requisite for electors of the most numerous branch of the State Legislature.

No person shall be a Representative who shall not have attained to the age of twenty-five years, and been seven years a citizen of the United States, and who shall not, when elected, be an inhabitant of that State in which he shall be chosen.

Representatives and direct taxes shall be apportioned among the several States which may be included within this Union according to their respective numbers, which shall be determined by adding to the whole number of free persons, including those bound to service for a term of years and excluding Indians not taxed, three-fifths of all other persons.

Section 2
HOUSE OF REPRESENTATIVES

Representatives shall have 2-year terms. They shall be elected by the people in the state. If a person can vote for the state representative, he or she can vote for the representative in Congress.

To be a representative, a person must be 25 years old, must have been a citizen of the United States for 7 years, and must live in the state she or he represents.

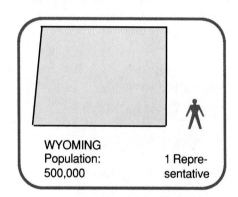

WYOMING
Population: 500,000

1 Representative

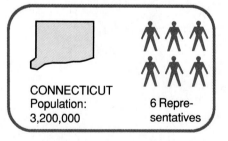

CONNECTICUT
Population: 3,200,000

6 Representatives

The number of representatives from each state depends on the number of people in that state. To find out how many representatives a state gets, count the number of free people; add three-fifths of the slaves; do not count Indians who are not taxed. [later changed]

We do count our people every 10 years in a national census. Years ending with 0 are census years.

The actual enumeration shall be made within three years after the first meeting of the Congress of the United States, and within every subsequent term of ten years, in such manner as they shall by law direct.

We shall count our people not more than 3 years after Congress first meets. Then we shall count them every 10 years. Congress shall say how to do this.

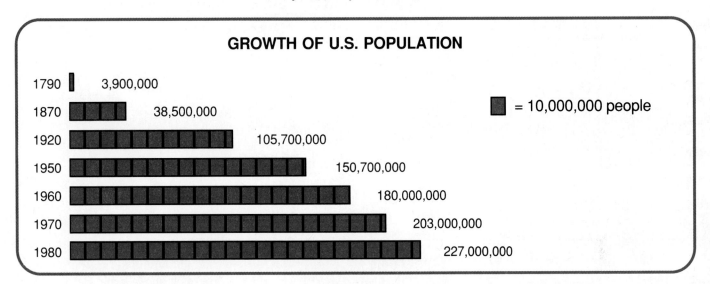

GROWTH OF U.S. POPULATION

Year	Population
1790	3,900,000
1870	38,500,000
1920	105,700,000
1950	150,700,000
1960	180,000,000
1970	203,000,000
1980	227,000,000

■ = 10,000,000 people

Congress set the top number of representatives at 435. Each representative's district now has about 525,000 people.

The number of Representatives shall not exceed one for every thirty thousand, but each state shall have at least one Representative; and until such enumeration shall be made, the State of New Hampshire shall be entitled to choose three; Massachusetts, eight; Rhode Island and Providence Plantations, one; Connecticut, five; New York, six; New Jersey, four; Pennsylvania, eight; Delaware, one; Maryland, six; Virginia, ten; North Carolina, five; South Carolina, five; and Georgia, three.

No representative's district shall be smaller than 30,000 people.

These add up to 65 representatives. Our first House had 65.

Representatives may not be appointed. They must be elected.

When vacancies happen in the representation from any State, the Executive Authority thereof shall issue writs of election to fill such vacancies.

If a representative dies or quits, the governor of that state shall call for an election.

The House can bring an official to trial. The Senate is the court. The Chief Justice is the judge.

This is the leader of the House of Representatives. The Vice President is leader of the Senate.

Impeach means "to call a person in office up for trial." It does not mean to remove him or her from office. The House first puts the charge in writing. The Senate is the court. It says whether the person being tried is guilty or not. Two-thirds of the senators present must find the person guilty to remove that person from office.

Only one President has been impeached. He was Andrew Johnson, in 1868. He kept office by one vote. Impeachment was begun against Richard Nixon in 1974. He resigned before the House could vote on his impeachment.

This was changed by the amendment passed in 1913. Senators are now elected by the people just as representatives are.

The Seventeenth Amendment changed this. The governor picks a person to serve until the people elect one. The Constitution reads this way because the state legislatures elected the United States senators before 1913. A senator may be appointed for as long as 2 years.

24

The House of Representatives shall choose their Speaker and other officers, and shall have the sole power of impeachment.

Section 3

The Senate of the United States shall be composed of two Senators from each State, chosen by the Legislature thereof, for six years; and each Senator shall have one vote.

Immediately after they shall be assembled in consequence of the first election, they shall be divided as equally as may be into three classes. The seats of the Senators of the first class shall be vacated at the expiration of the second year, of the second class at the expiration of the fourth year, and of the third class at the expiration of the sixth year, so that one-third may be chosen every second year; and if vacancies happen by resignation, or otherwise, during the recess of the Legislature of any State, the Executive thereof may make temporary appointments until the next meeting of the Legislature, which shall then fill such vacancies.

The House of Representatives shall pick its Speaker, or leader, and other officers. Only the House may call a person up for trial before the Senate.

Section 3
THE SENATE

Each state gets two senators in the Senate. The people elect them. They have 6-year terms. Each senator has one vote.

Senators are to be elected so that we do not have all new senators every 6 years. The terms of one-third will start when another one-third still has 4 years to go and the other one-third still has 2 years to go. Only one-third of the senators will be new, then, every 2 years.

If a state loses a senator in some way, the governor of that state will pick a person to serve until the people elect a new senator.

The Vice President of the United States is also President of the Senate.

The Senators pick someone to be temporary President of the Senate when the Vice President is away.

This means that the Senate cannot put them into jail or fine them. They can be tried later in court and fined or jailed.

No person shall be a Senator who shall not have attained to the age of thirty years, and been nine years a citizen of the United States, and who shall not, when elected, be an inhabitant of that State for which he shall be chosen.

The Vice President of the United States shall be President of the Senate, but shall have no vote unless they be equally divided.

The Senate shall choose their other officers, and also a President *pro tempore,* in the absence of the Vice President, or when he shall exercise the office of President of the United States.

The Senate shall have the sole power to try all impeachments. When sitting for that purpose, they shall be on oath or affirmation. When the President of the United States is tried, the Chief Justice shall preside; and no person shall be convicted without the concurrence of two-thirds of the members present. Judgment in cases of impeachment shall not extend further than to removal from office and disqualification to hold and enjoy any office of honor, trust, or profit under the United States; but the party convicted shall nevertheless be liable and subject to indictment, trial, judgment, and punishment, according to law.

To be a senator, a person must be 30 years old, must have been a citizen for 9 years, and must live in the state he or she represents.

The Vice President shall be President of the Senate. The Vice President votes only when the Senate has a tie vote.

The Senate shall elect its other officers. Senators shall pick a person to serve as temporary President of the Senate, who will be the leader when the Vice President is not there.

Only the Senate can try people whom the House of Representatives impeaches. The senators shall be under oath. The Chief Justice will run the trial if the President is impeached. No person shall be found guilty unless two-thirds of the senators at the trial agree to the charges.

Those who are impeached and whom the Senate finds guilty lose their jobs and may not again hold government jobs.

If the guilty person has broken the law, she or he may have to go before other courts.

Section 4

Before 1842, all representatives were elected by all the voters in a state. Since 1842, representatives have been elected by the voters of their districts.

The times, places, and man-ner of holding elections for Senators and Representatives shall be prescribed in each State by the Legislature thereof; but the Congress may at any time by law make or alter such regulations, except as to the places of choosing Senators.

This was put in so that no President could ever run the nation without Congress.

The Twentieth Amendment changed the meeting date to January 3.

The Congress shall assemble at least once in every year, and such meeting shall be on the first Monday in December, unless they shall by law appoint a different day.

Section 4
ELECTIONS AND MEETINGS

The state legislatures shall say when, where, and how the elections for senators and representatives shall be run. Congress may make laws that take the place of state laws about these elections. Congress may not change the places for choosing senators, though.

Congress must meet at least once a year. This meeting shall be on the first Monday in December. Congress may make a law to change this day. [changed to January 3]

Section 5

If there is an argument about who has won an election, the Senate or the House decides, not the courts.

Each House shall be the judge of the elections, returns, and qualifications of its own members, and a majority of each shall constitute a quorum to do business; but a smaller number may adjourn from day to day and may be authorized to compel the attendance of absent members in such manner and under such penalties as each House may provide.

According to this first clause, each house is free to make its own rules. That is why representatives can be limited in the length of debate, but senators cannot be.

Every word spoken in the House or Senate is now taken down by stenographers. *The Congressional Record* prints the proceedings of the House and the Senate.

Sometimes the House and Senate may hold secret meetings about our nation's safety.

Each House may determine the rules of its proceedings, punish its members for disorderly behavior, and, with the concurrence of two-thirds, expel a member.

Each House shall keep a journal of its proceedings and from time to time publish the same, excepting such parts as may in their judgment require secrecy;

Section 5
WHAT THE HOUSE CAN OR MUST DO

The House and the Senate have the right to say if their members are qualified and have been properly elected. If over half the members of the House or Senate are there, they can do their work. If less than half, they may delay the meeting until they get others to come in. The Senate and House may make their own rules about making absent members attend.

The Senate and House may make their own rules. Each house may punish its members if they do not behave properly. Each house may remove a member if two-thirds of the members vote for it.

The House and the Senate shall keep a record of what they do and say. They shall print this record. They need not print what should be secret.

26

If one house could stop meeting when it pleased, it could block all work of Congress. Both houses have to agree to stop meetings.

They can pass a bill to fix their salaries. The President must sign the bill. Representatives and senators now get $75,000 plus travel expenses to and from Washington. The salary has been changed from time to time because of changes in living costs.

If nothing were paid, only rich people could afford to be senators or representatives.

Members of Congress are not above the law. They can be punished for breaking laws, as all of us can be.

So they are not afraid to speak against the President, for example. Nobody can punish representatives or senators for what they say in their meetings.

The Constitution writers did not want members of Congress to make jobs for themselves.

and the yeas and nays of the members of either House on any question shall, at the desire of one-fifth of those present, be entered on the journal.

Neither House, during the session of Congress, shall, without the consent of the other, adjourn for more than three days, nor to any other place than that in which the two Houses shall be sitting.

Section 6

The Senators and Representatives shall receive a compensation for their services, to be ascertained by law and paid out of the Treasury of the United States. They shall in all cases, except treason, felony and breach of the peace, be privileged from arrest during their attendance at the session of their respective Houses, and in going to and returning from the same; and for any speech or debate in either House they shall not be questioned in any other place.

No Senator or Representative shall, during the time for which he was elected, be appointed to any civil office under the authority of the United States which shall have been created, or the emoluments whereof shall have been increased during such time; and no person holding any office under the United States shall be a member of either House during his continuance in office.

If one-fifth of the members present ask it, the record of how each member voted shall be kept.

Neither the House nor the Senate may stop meeting for more than 3 days unless the other House agrees. They may not have meetings separately in other places.

Section 6
RIGHTS AND DUTIES OF MEMBERS

Senators and representatives shall be paid for their work. The law shall fix their salaries. The United States Treasury shall pay the salaries. While senators and representatives are meeting or going to and from meetings, they shall not be arrested except for treason, serious crimes, or breaking the peace.

No one else may punish them for what they may say in their meetings.

Senators and representatives may not take another government job that is a new job started while they were in Congress. They may not take a different job if the salary for the job has been raised while they were in Congress.

Senators and representatives may hold no other government jobs while they are in Congress.

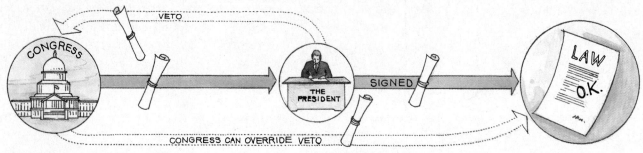

HOW A BILL BECOMES A LAW

This is how a bill becomes a law.

Section 7

Section 7
HOW TO MAKE LAWS

The Constitution writers wanted to be sure the people would have plenty to say about taxes. Therefore, they put the taxing power into the hands of the House members. The people could vote the House members out of office.

The writers wanted to make it very clear how we would get our laws. They did it this way to keep out hasty or unwise laws. If Congress wants a law the President does not like, the President can stop it with this veto power. Congress can override the veto if enough members vote for the bill a second time. The bill then becomes law.

All bills for raising revenue shall originate in the House of Representatives, but the Senate may propose or concur with amendments, as on other bills.

Every bill which shall have passed the House of Representatives and the Senate shall, before it becomes a law, be presented to the President of the United States; if he approve, he shall sign it, but if not, he shall return it, with his objections, to that House in which it shall have originated, who shall enter the objections at large on their journal and proceed to reconsider it. If after such reconsideration two-thirds of that House shall agree to pass the bill, it shall be sent, together with the objections, to the other House, by which it shall likewise be reconsidered; and if approved by two-thirds of that House, it shall become a law. But in all such cases the votes of both houses shall be determined by yeas and nays, and the names of the persons voting for and against the bill shall be entered on the journal of each House respectively.

Only the House of Representatives can introduce tax bills. The Senate can offer or agree with amendments to tax bills.

To become a law, a bill must pass the House and the Senate. Then it is sent to the President. If the President agrees, the bill is signed into law. If the President does not agree, the bill is sent back to the house it came from. The President must say why he did not sign the bill. The reasons are written into the records. The house goes over the bill again. If two-thirds of the members still vote for the bill, they send it to the other house with the President's objections. Now this house goes over the bill again. If two-thirds of this house votes for the bill again, it becomes a law. Each house must write which members voted "yes" and which voted "no."

Suppose Congress is about to adjourn and the President holds a bill without signing it. This is called a *pocket veto*. The President does not often use it.

The Constitution writers put this in so Congress could never bypass the President.

These are taxes that Congress can use to get money. Under the Articles of Confederation, Congress had no power to use these taxes.

If any bill shall not be returned by the President within ten days (Sundays excepted) after it shall have been presented to him, the same shall be a law in like manner as if he had signed it, unless the Congress by their adjournment prevent its return, in which case it shall not be a law.

Every order, resolution, or vote to which the concurrence of the Senate and House of Representatives may be necessary (except on a question of adjournment) shall be presented to the President of the United States; and before the same shall take effect, shall be approved by him, or being disapproved by him, shall be repassed by two-thirds of the Senate and House of Representatives, according to the rules and limitations prescribed in the case of a bill.

Section 8

The Congress shall have power:

To lay and collect taxes, duties, imposts, and excises;

If the President does not send back a bill within 10 days (not counting Sundays), the bill becomes a law, but only if Congress is still meeting.

Any action by one house that needs agreement by the other house must be reported to the President (except a move to stop meetings). The President must agree, or both houses must have a two-thirds vote for the move.

Section 8
WHAT CONGRESS SHALL DO

Congress shall have power to tax.

Congress has the power to tax.

Congress can spend money to (1) pay what the government owes; (2) form an army and a navy; (3) pay for what people need. This "general welfare" part lets Congress spend money as it pleases.

to pay the debts and provide for the common defense and general welfare of the United States;

Congress shall have power to pay what the nation owes. Congress may do what it needs to in order to protect us. It may do what needs to be done for our common good.

but all duties, imposts, and excises shall be uniform throughout the United States;

All taxes shall be the same in all parts of the United States.

This is how our nation can go into debt. In 1985, our nation owed $1.7 trillion.

To borrow money on the credit of the United States;

Congress may borrow money on our nation's promise to pay back.

Congress has made many laws about business and labor. Congress has used this power to protect civil rights in jobs, housing, and schooling. The Civil Rights Act of 1964 is an example. These few words give Congress the power to pass laws about almost anything the people need. They also keep states from making laws about goods moving between states. These words also help tie our states together into one nation.

To regulate commerce with foreign nations, and among the several States, and with the Indian Tribes;

Congress shall make the rules about trade with other nations, trade between states, and trade with the Indians.

To establish an uniform rule of naturalization and uniform laws on the subject of bankruptcies throughout the United States;

Congress shall make one set of rules so a person from another nation may become an American citizen. Congress shall have power to make the same laws for all states about people who cannot pay what they owe.

One of the hardest jobs Congress has is to decide who can become a citizen of the United States.

To coin money, regulate the value thereof, and of foreign coin,

Congress shall have power to stamp or print money and to say how much it shall be worth. Congress can shut out money of other nations.

When the states used different money, there was trouble. These words make it clear that only Congress can mint or print money.

Congress has the power to stamp or print money.

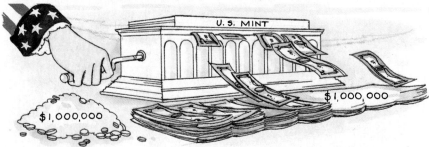

You need to use the same way of measuring things in a nation.

and fix the standard of weights and measures;

Congress may decide how we shall weigh and measure things.

To provide for the punishment of counterfeiting the securities and current coin of the United States;

Congress shall make laws to punish those who make fake government bonds, bills, or stamps.

At the time, there were about 75 post offices in the 13 states. There are now about 31,000.

To establish post offices and post roads;

Congress shall set up post offices and have roads built.

Congress has the power to build post offices and roads.

An inventor who takes out a patent may keep the right to his or her invention for a certain number of years. Authors may keep the right to their works for a certain number of years.

To promote the progress of science and useful arts by securing for limited times to authors and inventors the exclusive right to their respective writings and discoveries;

Congress shall help science and learning grow by giving patents and copyrights to inventors and authors.

Below the Supreme Court are the courts of appeal and the district courts. Each state also has its own courts.

To constitute tribunals inferior to the Supreme Court;

Congress shall set up courts lower than the Supreme Court.

Congress has the power to set up courts lower than the Supreme Court.

THE FEDERAL COURT SYSTEM

We used to have trouble with pirates.

Because we had become a nation, only Congress should have this power. If each state had the power, any state could get all other states into trouble or even into a war.

Only Congress can declare war. It was Congress that declared war against Japan after the Pearl Harbor attack on December 7, 1941. Some Presidents have taken over Congress's war powers by calling wars by another name. The Korean war, for example, was called a police action. The Vietnam War was called a peacekeeping mission. After the Vietnam War, Congress made its power clear by passing the War Powers Resolution. This law is meant to keep a President from sending troops on his own without keeping Congress informed.

Letters of marque were letters given to people by the government saying that they might use ships to fight the enemy or take enemy property.

The Constitution lets each state have soldiers, which were called *militia*. They are now called the National Guard.

To define and punish pi-racies and felonies com-mitted on the high seas, and offenses against the law of nations;

To declare war, grant letters of marque and repri-sal, and make rules concern-ing captures on land and water;

To raise and support armies, but no appropri-ation of money to that use shall be for a longer term than two years;

To provide and maintain a navy;

To make rules for the government and regulation of the land and naval forces;

To provide for calling forth the militia to execute the laws of the Union, sup-press insurrections, and re-pel invasions;

Congress shall say what are crimes on American ships sailing outside the United States. Congress shall say what are crimes against international law. Congress shall say how these crimes are to be punished.

Congress shall say when we are at war. It shall have the power to tell soldiers they may fight our enemy or take enemy property. It shall make rules about taking enemy property on land or sea.

Congress shall have the power to raise an army and pay the soldiers. Congress may keep an army for only 2 years at a time.

Congress shall start and keep a navy.

Congress shall make rules to keep the army and navy in order.

Congress shall be able to call on help from a state's soldiers for three reasons: to keep the nation's laws; to fight rebels against the government; to fight enemies who attack our nation.

Congress has the power to raise an army.

To provide for organizing, arming, and disciplining the militia, and for governing such part of them as may be employed in the service of the United States, reserving to the States respectively the appointment of the officers and the authority of training the militia according to the discipline prescribed by Congress;

Congress shall see to it that groups of state soldiers, or militia, are formed and are given arms and rules. Congress shall make rules about how they shall serve the country. The states shall pick the militia officers. The states shall train the militia according to Congress's rules.

During the Revolutionary War, the British chased Congress from place to place. Therefore, Congress wanted to find a place for the new government. It was not to be a part of any state. So the District of Columbia was formed. Today 630,000 people live there. They have a mayor and a city council. They have no governor nor any voting member in the House or Senate.

To exercise exclusive legislation in all cases whatsoever over such district (not exceeding ten miles square) as may, by cession of particular States and the acceptance of Congress, become the seat of the Government of the United States, and to exercise like authority over all places purchased by the consent of the Legislature of the State in which the same shall be, for the erection of forts, magazines, arsenals, dockyards, and other needful buildings; —And

Congress shall make all laws for the place in which it meets (Washington, DC). Congress shall govern all places that it buys from states for forts, storing arms, ship docks, and other buildings.

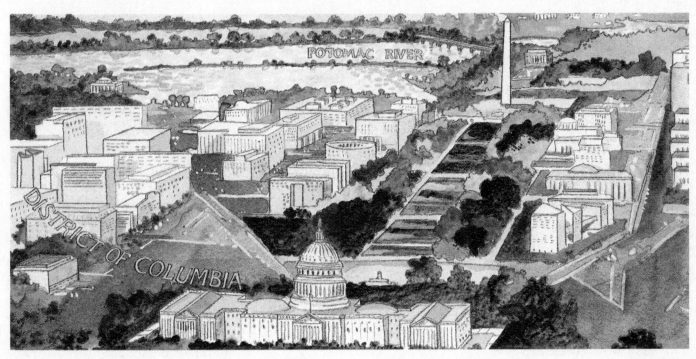

POTOMAC RIVER

DISTRICT OF COLUMBIA

These words show how much power Congress has. Members of Congress can make *all* laws they think we need.

To make all laws which shall be necessary and proper for carrying into execution the foregoing powers, and all other powers vested by this Constitution in the Government of the United States, or in any department or officer thereof.

Congress shall have power to make the laws it needs to use the powers listed in Section 8. Congress may also make laws for other powers given in the Constitution.

Section 8 listed things that Congress may do. Section 9 lists 10 things that Congress may not do.

Section 9

Section 9
WHAT CONGRESS SHALL NOT DO

"Persons" meant slaves. The writers of the Constitution wanted to stop more slaves from coming in after 1808.

The migration or importation of such persons as any of the States now existing shall think proper to admit shall not be prohibited by the Congress prior to the year one thousand eight hundred and eight, but a tax or duty may be imposed on such importation, not exceeding ten dollars for each person.

The different states may bring in as many slaves as they want until 1808, but Congress may tax them up to $10 for each person brought in.

People being held in jail must be brought to court and told why they are being held.

A writ of habeas corpus is an order that is issued by a court. *Habeas corpus* means "you should have the body." Such an order requires a police officer holding a person in jail to bring this person before a court. Here the person must be told why she or he is being held.

The privilege of the writ of habeas corpus shall not be suspended, unless when in cases of rebellion or invasion the public safety may require it.

All imprisoned persons must be told the reason for their being held. The court then decides if this is reason enough to continue to hold them. This holds true unless the country is in danger or martial law is in force.

A bill of attainder in Britain was a special act of Parliament. By it a person could be called guilty and be put to death without a jury, without a court hearing, and without real proof of guilt.

Ex post facto means "after the fact." People may not be punished for what they did before a law was passed.

No bill of attainder or ex post facto law shall be passed.

Congress may not provide for punishment of a person without a judicial trial. Congress may not pass a law that will punish a person for something that was not against the law when the person did it.

34

This means a flat tax on each person. However, the Sixteenth Amendment calls for a different and fairer tax.	No capitation or other direct tax shall be laid, unless in proportion to the census or enumeration here-in before directed to be taken.	Congress may not tax a person a flat sum unless all are taxed the same sum.
The farm states were afraid Congress might tax the grain they sent out of the country.	No tax or duty shall be laid on articles exported from any state.	Congress shall not tax products sent from a state.
This keeps Congress from favoring one state over another.	No preference shall be given by any regulation of commerce or revenue to the ports of one State over those of another, nor shall vessels bound to or from one State be obliged to enter, clear, or pay duties in another.	Congress shall make no laws about trade that will favor one state over another. Ships going from one state to another shall not pay taxes in order to do so.
This keeps the President from spending money without an okay from Congress.	No money shall be drawn from the Treasury but in consequence of appropriations made by law; and a regular statement and account of the receipts and expenditures of all public money shall be published from time to time.	No one may spend any government money unless both houses pass a bill to do so and the President signs it. Congress must let the people know how much money has come in and been spent.

No U.S. official or government employee may accept a noble title from a foreign government.

	No title of nobility shall be granted by the United States. And no person holding any office of profit or trust under them shall, without the consent of the Congress, accept of any present, emolument, office, or title of any kind whatever from any king, prince, or foreign state.	The government shall not give any noble titles to people (such as duke, baron, earl). No person working for our government may take a title, a present, pay, or a job from another nation unless Congress agrees.
These are powers given to Congress in Section 8. Because the states had these powers under the Articles of Confederation, the government was weak.	**Section 10** No State shall enter into any treaty, alliance, or confederation; grant letters of marque and reprisal; coin money; emit bills of credit;	**Section 10** WHAT THE STATES MAY NOT DO No state shall make a treaty or tie itself up with another nation. No state may give people the right to fight or work against other nations. No state may have its own money.

35

This part stops the states from dealing with other nations. Before the Constitution was written, the different states passed laws that fouled up private agreements and contracts. Now the states could no longer do so.

make anything but gold and silver coin a tender in payment of debts; pass any bill of attainder, ex post facto law, or law impairing the obligation of contracts; or grant any title of nobility.

No State shall, without the consent of the Congress, lay any imposts or duties on imports or exports, except what may be absolutely necessary for executing its inspection laws, and the net produce of all duties and imposts, laid by any State on imports or exports, shall be for the use of the Treasury of the United States; and all such laws shall be subject to the revision and control of the Congress.

No State shall, without the consent of Congress, lay any duty of tonnage, keep troops or ships of war in time of peace, enter into any agreement or compact with another State or with a foreign power, or engage in war, unless actually invaded or in such imminent danger as will not admit of delay.

No state may use anything but gold and silver for money. No state may condemn a person to death without a jury trial and witnesses. No state may punish a person for something not wrong when he or she did it. No state may make a law to wipe out written agreements made in the right way. No state may give a person a noble title.

Unless Congress agrees, no state may put taxes on goods coming in or going out of a state, except to keep its inspection laws working. This tax money shall go to the national government. Congress may change any such state tax law.

No state may tax ships. No state may keep an army (except state militia). No state may keep warships in peacetime. No state may make agreements with another state or with a foreign nation unless Congress agrees. No state may go to war unless it is attacked and cannot delay fighting.

No state may make a treaty with a foreign nation.

No state may go to war unless it is attacked.

Section 1

1. Why does the Constitution say that only Congress shall make our nation's laws?

2. Why does the Constitution call for a Congress with two houses?

Section 2

3. Are the qualifications for a representative sensible? Why, or why not?

4. Why did Southern states want to count slaves as a part of the population? Why did Northern states think this was not fair? How would you have settled the argument?

5. Why does the Constitution call for a count, or census, of our population every 10 years? Why not every year? Why not every 20 years?

6. Why have we had to change the way in which a state gets more or fewer representatives?

7. Why do you think Congress set the number of representatives at 435?

8. Why do you think the Constitution writers did not permit a state governor to appoint a representative to replace one who had resigned or died?

9. Why do you think the Constitution writers did not say who should become leader of the House of Representatives?

10. Why do you think the Constitution writers gave impeachment power to the House rather than to the Senate?

Section 3

11. Why do you think the Seventeenth Amendment was added to change the way senators are elected?

12. Why are all senators not elected at the same time?

13. Why do you think the qualifications for a senator were made higher than those for a representative?

14. Why do you think impeachment is so complicated? Why should there be a two-thirds vote instead of a simple majority?

Section 4

15. Why did the Constitution writers say that Congress must meet at least once a year?

Section 5

16. Why does the Constitution require that more than half of the House and Senate members be present to do business?

17. Why does the Constitution require the House and Senate to keep a record of what they do and say? Why should the record be printed?

18. Why may the two houses not stop their meetings unless both agree?

Section 6

19. Do you think members of Congress should be paid for their work? Why, or why not?

20. Why does the Constitution say that members of Congress should not be questioned about what they say in meetings?

21. Why should members of Congress not be able to take jobs that were started while they were in Congress?

22. Why should members of Congress not be allowed to hold other government jobs?

Section 7

23. Why was only the House of Representatives given power to write tax bills?

24. How does a bill become a law? Why were all these steps put into the Constitution?

25. How did the Constitution writers use the President's veto power to prevent unwise or hasty laws?

26. How did the writers prevent the President from stopping passage of any law he did not happen to like?

Section 8

27. Why was it important for the Constitution to say plainly that the government would pay its debts?

28. What are the three reasons for which Congress may spend money? Why do you think the writers put this rule into the Constitution?

29. Do you think Congress should have power to borrow money and get the nation into debt? Give reasons for your answer.

30. Why do you think Congress, and not the states, should have power to control trade?

31. Why should only Congress have the right to mint and print money?

32. Why did the Constitution writers think it was important to protect the rights of inventors and authors?

33. Why should the states not have the right to make their own systems of weights and measures?

34. Why do you think the Constitution writers gave the power to declare war only to Congress? Why did Congress pass the War Powers Resolution?

35. Why was the power of Congress to keep an army held down to 2 years?

36. Why should Congress have power over the state militia?

37. Why do you think the writers did not put the meeting place of Congress in one of the states?

Section 9

38. What power did the Constitution give Congress over the slave trade? Why did the Constitution writers not stop the slave trade at once?

39. What is habeas corpus? Why is it important enough to be in the Constitution?

40. Why is an ex post facto law unfair?

41. Is a poll tax fair? Why, or why not?

42. Why should one state not have to pay a tax on goods from another state?

43. Why should Congress have to let the people know how much public money has been taken in and spent?

44. Why does the Constitution say the government may not give titles of nobility?

Section 10

45. Why should separate states not be able to make treaties with other nations?

46. Why do you think the Constitution writers listed so many things a state may not do?

ARTICLE II

Section 1

The writers had many arguments about how much power should be given to a President. We now have Presidents with a great deal of power.

The Electoral College is confusing. The Constitution writers thought the people were not smart enough to vote for a President. So the writers had them vote for electors. These electors would then elect a President. Now, although the people of each state still choose their electors, the political parties make their own choices of persons to run for President and Vice President. They do this at their national conventions sometime before November in an election year. At the time of the election, each ballot must carry either the names of the candidates for President and Vice President or the names of the electors or both. Then the people vote.

The Executive power shall be vested in a President of the United States of America. He shall hold his office during the term of four years, and, together with the Vice President, chosen for the same term, be elected as follows:

Each State shall appoint, in such manner as the Legislature thereof may direct, a number of electors, equal to the whole number of Senators and Representatives to which the State may be entitled in the Congress; but no Senator or Representative or person holding an office of trust or profit under the United States shall be appointed an elector.

The electors shall meet in their respective States and vote by ballot for two persons, of whom one at least shall not be an inhabitant of the same State

ARTICLE II
EXECUTIVE DEPARTMENT

Section 1
THE PRESIDENT AND VICE PRESIDENT

The leader of our government shall be a President. The President and a Vice President shall have 4-year terms. This is the way they shall be elected:

Each state shall elect electors to vote for President. Each state gets as many electors as the state has senators plus representatives.

No senator or representative may be an elector. Nobody holding a government job may be an elector.

The electors meet in their own states. They each vote for two people. At least one of the two must be from a different state.

Presidential candidates are officially nominated at their party's national convention.

According to the Constitution, they are voting for the electors, but they know the electors will then vote for the party candidates. Therefore, when the November election is over, it is generally known who is going to be President. The electors have always voted as expected.

Electors meet in their own states in December and cast their ballots. These ballots are then sent to Washington, where they are opened and counted before a joint session of Congress in the House of Representatives.

For many years, some people have suggested that this method of electing our President and our Vice President be changed. They feel it is no longer necessary to have an Electoral College.

All this was changed in 1804 by the adoption of the Twelfth Amendment. See the Twelfth Amendment (pp. 58–60).

This arrangement was changed because in 1800, Thomas Jefferson and Aaron Burr each received the same number of electoral votes. It took 36 ballots in the House of Representatives before Jefferson was elected.

with themselves. And they shall make a list of all the persons voted for and of the number of votes for each, which list they shall sign and certify and transmit, sealed, to the seat of the Government of the United States, directed to the President of the Senate. The President of the Senate shall, in the presence of the Senate and House of Representatives, open all the certificates, and the votes shall then be counted. The person having the greatest number of votes shall be the President, if such number be a majority of the whole number of electors appointed; and if there be more than one who have such majority and have an equal number of votes, then the House of Representatives shall immediately choose by ballot one of them for President; and if

Then they make a list of all the people whom they have voted for. After each name, they write the number of votes that person got. They sign this list. They seal it and send it to the President of the Senate at the capital. The list is opened in front of the Senate and the House. The votes are counted. The person getting the greatest number of votes becomes President if more than half of all the electors voted for that person. If there is a tie vote and more than one person has more than half the electors for them, the House of Representatives elects one of them. If

IN 1800, THOMAS JEFFERSON AND AARON BURR RECEIVED THE SAME NUMBER OF ELECTORAL VOTES FOR PRESIDENT.

IT TOOK 36 VOTES IN THE HOUSE OF REPRESENTATIVES TO BREAK THE TIE. JEFFERSON WAS FINALLY ELECTED PRESIDENT.

Congress did pick the day in 1872. The day would be the Tuesday after the first Monday in November in every fourth year.

NOVEMBER 1988						
SUN.	MON.	TUES.	WED.	THURS.	FRI.	SAT.
		1	2	3	4	5
6	7	8	9	10	11	12
13	14	15	16	17	18	19
20	21	22	23	24	25	26
27	28	29	30			

Election Day

no person have a majority, then from the five highest on the list the said House shall in like manner choose the President. But in choosing the President, the votes shall be taken by States, the representation from each State having one vote. A quorum, for this purpose, shall consist of a member or members from two-thirds of the States, and a majority of all the States shall be necessary to a choice. In every case, after the choice of the President, the person having the greatest number of votes of the electors shall be the Vice President. But if there should remain two or more who have equal votes, the Senate shall choose from them by ballot the Vice President.

The Congress may determine the time of choosing the electors and the day on which they shall give their votes, which day shall be the same throughout the United States.

No person except a natural born citizen, or a citizen of United States at the time of the adoption of this Constitution, shall be eligible to the office of President; neither shall any person be eligible to that office who shall not have attained to the age of thirty-five years and been fourteen years a resident within the United States.

nobody has more than half the electoral voters, the House of Representatives votes for one of the five highest on the list. But in voting for the President, the votes shall go by states. Each state now gets only one vote. At least one person must be there from two-thirds of the states. The winner must get more than half of these state votes. Always, after the President has been chosen, the person having the second-highest electoral vote shall be Vice President. If there is a tie electoral vote, the Senate shall elect the Vice President.

Congress may say when the states shall elect their electors. Congress may pick the day when the electoral votes shall come in. They shall pick the same day for all the states.

The President must be born in the United States or born of citizens of the United States, or the President must have been a citizen at the time the Constitution started working. He or she must be 35 years old. The President must have lived in the United States for at least 14 years.

PRESIDENTIAL LINE OF SUCCESSION

In 1886, Congress made a law that if both the President and the Vice President cannot work, the Secretary of State was next in line, followed by other Cabinet members.

In 1947, the law was changed. Under the new law, the Speaker of the House and the temporary President of the Senate were placed ahead of the members of the Cabinet.

In 1967, Congress changed the law by passing the Twenty-fifth Amendment. If the Vice President becomes President, the new President can appoint someone to be Vice President. Both houses of Congress must approve the appointment.

In case of the removal of the President from office, or of his death, resignation, or inability to discharge the powers and duties of the said office, the same shall devolve on the Vice President, and the Congress may by law provide for the case of removal, death, resignation, or inability, both of the President and Vice President, declaring what officer shall then act as President, and such officer shall act accordingly until the disability be removed or a President shall be elected.

If the President cannot do the work, the Vice President shall take over. If both President and Vice President cannot work, Congress shall say who is to do the work. This person shall work until the President or Vice President can once more do it or until a new President is elected.

In 1789, the President's pay was set at $25,000 a year. The President's salary is now set at $200,000; the Vice President's is $97,900.

The President shall, at stated times, receive for his services a compensation which shall neither be increased nor diminished during the period for which he shall have been elected, and he shall not receive within that period any other emolument from the United States, or any of them.

The President shall be paid for working. The pay shall not be raised or lowered during the time the President is in office. The President may not take any other pay from the government. The President may not take pay from any state.

Andrew Jackson is speaking to the people on the way to his swearing in. On his inauguration day, 10,000 people went to Washington to celebrate.

After Warren G. Harding's death in office, Calvin Coolidge was sworn in. Coolidge's father, a justice of the peace, swore him in at 2:47 a.m. in his own home in Plymouth, Vermont.

John F. Kennedy became President in the normal way, by being elected to the office. He was sworn in in Washington, DC, by Chief Justice Earl Warren.

Lyndon B. Johnson was sworn in as President on the presidential plane after Kennedy was killed in Dallas, Texas. He was sworn in by federal judge Sarah T. Hughes.

This oath is usually given by the Chief Justice of the Supreme Court on January 20.

Before he enter on the execution of his office he shall take the following oath or affirmation: "I do solemnly swear (or affirm) that I will faithfully execute the office of President of the United States, and will, to the best of my ability, preserve, protect, and defend the Constitution of the United States."

Before the President starts to work, the President must swear to do it faithfully. The President swears to keep, protect, and fight for the Constitution.

These words give the President great power in wartime. In World War II, President Roosevelt used this power to give orders. During the Vietnam War, Presidents Johnson and Nixon fought with Congress about the war. Congress tried to limit this power by limiting how much money could be spent in Vietnam.

The President has never personally led the army or navy in a war. The Secretary of Defense usually carries out the President's orders.

This means one of the Cabinet. There are now 13 departments in the Cabinet. They meet to advise the President.

The President can sign a treaty, but the Senate must agree by a two-thirds vote. After World War I, President Wilson signed a treaty to end the war. The Senate voted it down.

Section 2

The President shall be Commander in Chief of the Army and Navy of the United States, and of the militia of the several States when called into the actual service of the United States; he may require the opinion, in writing, of the principal officer in each of the executive departments upon any subject relating to the duties of their respective offices, and he shall have power to grant reprieves and pardons for offenses against the United States, except in cases of impeachment.

He shall have power, by and with the advice and consent of the Senate, to make treaties, provided two-thirds of the Senators present concur; and he shall nominate and by and with the advice and consent of the Senate shall appoint ambassadors, other public ministers and consuls, judges of the Supreme Court, and all other officers of the United States whose appointments are not herein otherwise provided for, and which shall be established by law; but the Congress may by law vest the appointment of such inferior officers as they think proper in the President alone, in the courts of law, or in the heads of departments.

Section 2
WHAT THE PRESIDENT SHALL DO

The President shall be leader of the army and navy. The President shall be leader of the state soldiers (militia) when the nation needs them.

The President may ask any members in the Cabinet questions about any part of their work.

The President shall have power to pardon anyone who has done something against the government, except those who are impeached.

The President may make treaties with other nations if two-thirds of the senators who are meeting vote for them.

The President, with the agreement of the Senate, shall pick people to represent our nation in other lands. In the same way, the President shall pick the Supreme Court judges. The President shall also pick all other officials who work for our federal government. The President shall also pick officials for jobs that may be needed in the future. Congress may make laws to let the President or the courts or the Cabinet members pick some of the people for the smaller jobs themselves.

43

The President shall have power to fill up all vacancies that may happen during the recess of the Senate by granting commissions, which shall expire at the end of their next session.

When the Senate is not meeting, the President may pick people for unfilled government jobs. These people stay in office until the Senate ends its next meeting.

Section 3

Section 3
WHAT THE PRESIDENT SHALL DO

The President usually does this in a speech to Congress when it meets in January. The President also sends special messages to Congress about important matters.

He shall from time to time give to the Congress information of the state of the Union and recommend to their consideration such measures as he shall judge necessary and expedient; he may, on extraordinary occasions convene both Houses, or either of them, and in case of disagreement between them with respect to the time of adjournment, he may adjourn them to such time as he shall think

The President shall sometimes tell Congress how things are going in the nation. The President shall say what needs to be done. When there is a great need, the President may call either house or the whole Congress together for a special meeting. If the two houses cannot agree about closing the meeting, the President may close the meeting.

The President meets with representatives of other nations.

Once a year, usually in January, the President gives a speech to Congress. In this speech, he discusses the state of the nation.

Only the President can recognize a new nation's government. The President may tell a foreign representative to go back home, too. The President is the only official voice for our government with other nations.

President Andrew Johnson was the only President to be impeached. He was not convicted. President Richard Nixon resigned under the threat of impeachment.

proper; he shall receive ambassadors and other public ministers; he shall take care that the laws be faithfully executed and shall commission all the officers of the United States.

Section 4

The President, Vice President, and all civil officers of the United States shall be removed from office on impeachment for and conviction of treason, bribery, or other high crimes and misdemeanors.

The President shall deal with representatives of other nations. The President shall see to it that the nation's laws are obeyed. The President shall pick the government officers.

Section 4
IMPEACHMENT

The President, Vice President, or other government officers may be brought up for trial before the Senate by the House. If they are guilty of working against our nation or of taking bribes or of doing other wrong, they shall be removed from office.

DISCUSSION: ARTICLE II

Section 1

1. Why did the Constitution writers create the Electoral College? Do you think they should have done so?

2. What changes did the Twelfth Amendment make in the way the President and Vice President are elected? Did these changes improve the rules? How?

3. Look at the Twentieth Amendment (pp. 67–69). What changes did the Twentieth Amendment make? Did these changes improve the rules? How?

4. Do you think we should get rid of the Electoral College? Why, or why not?

5. Would you change any of the qualifications for the presidency? If so, why?

6. What do you think is the best line of succession if something should happen to the President and Vice President?

Section 2

7. Do you think the President should be Commander in Chief of the army and navy during wartime? Why, or why not?

8. Why does the Constitution say that the Senate must agree to treaties the President makes? Do you think the rule will always turn out well? How could it have bad results?

9. Why do you think the writers of the Constitution had the President pick the Supreme Court judges? Why should Congress not pick them? Why should they not be elected by the people?

Section 3

10. Why should the President have to speak to Congress about the state of the nation?

11. Why do you think the President might need to call Congress together?

· THE SUPREME COURT ·

The Constitution left the size of the Supreme Court up to Congress. In 1789, Congress decided on a Chief Justice and five other judges. John Jay became our first Chief Justice. The Supreme Court now has a Chief Justice and eight other judges.

There are 13 circuit courts of appeals with 168 circuit judges and 94 district courts with 575 district judges. The United States district courts rule in cases in which our national government's laws may have been broken. They also rule in cases that involve citizens of different states. The Supreme Court takes cases between states. The Supreme Court also judges cases that come up first in the state courts or lower government courts if there is still a question about the decision in view of what the Constitution says.

ARTICLE III

Section 1

The judicial power of the United States shall be vested in one Supreme Court, and in such inferior courts as the Congress may from time to time ordain and establish.

ARTICLE III
JUDICIAL DEPARTMENT

Section 1
GOVERNMENT COURTS

A Supreme Court shall have the judging power. Congress may set up lower courts also.

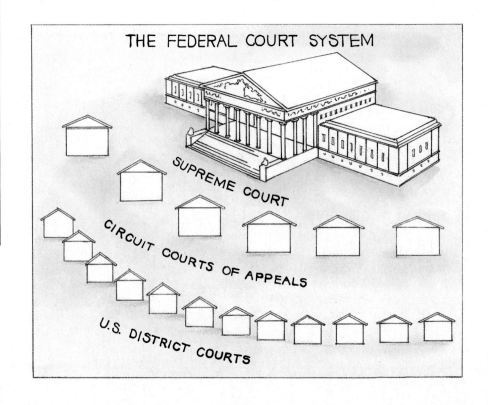

THE FEDERAL COURT SYSTEM

SUPREME COURT

CIRCUIT COURTS OF APPEALS

U.S. DISTRICT COURTS

The President picks all United States judges. The Senate approves them. They may keep their jobs for life unless they lose them by impeachment. The Chief Justice is paid $104,000.

The judges, both of the Supreme and inferior courts, shall hold their offices during good behavior, and shall at stated times receive for their services a compensation which shall not be diminished during their continuance in office.

The judges of all United States courts shall stay in office so long as they do no crimes. They shall be paid for their work. Their pay shall not be lowered while they are in office.

Section 2

Section 2
CASES FOR GOVERNMENT COURTS

The Constitution writers argued a lot about the powers of the President and of Congress. They argued very little about the power of the courts. The greatest power the Supreme Court has is to review laws passed by Congress or by a state. The Court decides if the Constitution permits the law or if it does not. This power is called the power of *judicial review*. It was declared to be a proper Supreme Court power in 1803 when Chief Justice Marshall wrote his famous opinion.

The judicial power shall extend to all cases in law and equity arising under this Constitution, the laws of the United States, and treaties made, or which shall be made, under their authority;

The government courts shall judge cases that: are about something in the Constitution; are about something in the nation's laws; are about government treaties;

to all cases affecting ambassadors, other public ministers, and consuls;

are about any government's representatives in the United States;

to all cases of admiralty and maritime jurisdiction;

are about sea laws;

to controversies to which the United States shall be a party;

come up when the United States government has to punish those who break the laws;

to controversies between two or more States,

are between states;

between a State and citizens of another State,

are between a state and a citizen of another state;

between citizens of different States,

are between people of different states;

between citizens of the same State claiming lands under grants of different States, and between a State, or the citizens thereof, and foreign states, citizens, or subjects.

are between people of the same state who claim lands in other states; are between a state or a United States citizen and a foreign nation or a foreign citizen.

47

Some people do not like some Supreme Court decisions. Sometimes the members of Congress try to pass laws to take away Supreme Court power. Congress can also pass new amendments to the Constitution that reverse specific Supreme Court decisions. This has been done four times. The Supreme Court must accept all amendments that are ratified.

The right to trial by jury

The British Parliament had often charged treason against a person they did not like. The Constitution writers wanted to keep this from happening here. This part of Section 3 prevents Congress from using treason to punish people whose politics they do not like.

Aaron Burr, Jefferson's Vice President from 1801 to 1805, was tried for treason and acquitted at a trial presided over by Chief Justice John Marshall in 1807.

In all cases affecting ambassadors, other public ministers and consuls, and those in which a State shall be party, the Supreme Court shall have original jurisdiction. In all the other cases before mentioned, the Supreme Court shall have appellate jurisdiction both as to law and fact, with such exceptions and under such regulations as the Congress shall make.

The trial of all crimes, except in cases of impeachment, shall be by jury, and such trial shall be held in the State where the said crimes shall have been committed; but when not committed within any State, the trial shall be at such place or places as the Congress may by law have directed.

Section 3

Treason against the United States shall consist only in levying war against them, or in adhering to their enemies, giving them aid and comfort. No person shall be convicted of treason unless on the testimony of two witnesses to the same overt act, or on confession in open court.

The Congress shall have power to declare the punishment of treason, but no attainder of treason shall work corruption of blood or forfeiture except during the life of the person attainted.

The case must first go to the Supreme Court if a foreign representative or a state is involved in the case.

All the other cases listed on page 47 must first go into lower courts. After the judge has ruled there, the case may go to the Supreme Court. Congress may make more rules about such cases.

Anybody who does a crime has a right to trial by jury. Impeached officers do not. The trial shall be held in the state where the person did the crime. If the crime was not done in any state, the trial shall be held wherever Congress says by law.

Section 3
TREASON

Treason means fighting against the United States or helping its enemies.

To prove treason, there must be two witnesses who both saw the person do wrong, or the person must admit it before the court.

Congress shall say what punishment a person gets for treason. But any punishment for treason must stop when that person dies. Children shall not be punished for the parent's treason.

DISCUSSION: ARTICLE III

Section 1

1. Why does the Supreme Court have an uneven number of judges?

2. Why do you think the Supreme Court judges are permitted to serve for life?

3. Do you think Supreme Court judges should have to retire at age 65 or 70? Why, or why not?

Section 2

4. Explain the power of judicial review.

5. Why is a trial by jury guaranteed?

6. Why should court cases be held in the state in which a crime has been committed?

Section 3

7. Why was Congress so careful about cases that involved treason?

8. Why did Congress want at least two witnesses to prove treason?

ARTICLE IV

ARTICLE IV
HOW THE STATES SHALL WORK TOGETHER

Section 1

Section 1
STATE RECORDS AND RULINGS

The Constitution writers wanted to make clear that we are one united nation. They therefore say here that a state has to honor what is legally done in another state. For example, if you sign a contract in New York, it is also good in California.

Full faith and credit shall be given in each State to the public acts, records, and judicial proceedings of every other State. **And the Congress may by general laws prescribe the manner in which such acts, records, and proceedings shall be proved, and the effect thereof.**

All states shall honor the laws, records, and court rulings of other states.

Congress may make laws to say how the laws, records, and court rulings shall be honored.

Section 2

Section 2
RIGHTS OF CITIZENS

This means that a state shall not favor its own citizens over the citizens of another state.

The citizens of each State shall be entitled to all privileges and immunities of citizens in the several States.

The rights you have as a United States citizen in your own state you shall have in all other states.

The Supreme Court has ruled that a governor does not always have to send the person back. Congress fixed no punishment for a state that does not send the person back. A state does not send a person back until it looks at the record. Also, the person may ask for a hearing in court before she or he is sent back.

A person charged in any State with treason, felony, or other crime, who shall flee from justice and be found in another State, shall, on demand of the Executive Authority of the State from which he fled, be delivered up, to be removed to the State having jurisdiction of the crime.

If a person has broken a law and runs away to another state, the governor shall send that person back if the other governor asks that it be done.

This part of the Constitution has no meaning now that we have no

No person held to service or labor in one State, under

Slaves do not become free by escaping to a free state. They

49

slaves. Without this part of the Constitution, the slave states would not have signed it.

the laws thereof, escaping into another, shall, in consequence of any law or regulation therein, be discharged from such service or labor, but shall be delivered up on claim of the party to whom such service or labor may be due.

shall be sent back to their owners.

Usually new states were first called *territories*. The people would write a constitution and Congress would consider it. When everything was all right, Congress would pass an act letting the new state in.

But in the Civil War, President Lincoln and Congress let the western part of Virginia become the new state of West Virginia. The people there were loyal to the Union. Lincoln wanted to strike back at the South by breaking Virginia into two states.

Section 3

New States may be admitted by the Congress into this Union; but no new State shall be formed or erected within the jurisdiction of any other State; nor any State be formed by the junction of two or more States, or parts of States, without the consent of the Legislatures of the States concerned, as well as of the Congress.

The Congress shall have power to dispose of and make all needful rules and regulations respecting the territory or other property belonging to the United States; and nothing in this Constitution shall be so construed as to prejudice any claims of the United States, or of any particular State.

Section 3
NEW STATES

Congress may bring new states into our nation. But a new state shall not be made inside an old one.

No new state shall be made by putting states or parts of states together unless the state legislatures and Congress agree.

Congress shall make rules about all government lands.

Some of the states still claimed western lands. When the Constitution was written, these claims had not yet been settled.

Nothing in the Constitution says anything about the land claims of the states now.

Section 4

The United States shall guarantee to every State in this Union a republican form of government, and shall protect each of them against invasion, and, on application of the Legislature, or of the Executive (when the Legislature cannot be convened), against domestic violence.

Section 4
RIGHTS OF STATES

The United States guarantees every state a republican form of government. The United States shall protect each state against enemy attack. If the state legislature or the governor calls for help, the President can send in soldiers to keep the peace within the state.

The colonists did not like the British system of having a king. They wanted to govern themselves. A republican government is one in which the people elect their leaders.

50

Section 1

1. Why should states honor the rulings and laws of other states?

Section 2

2. Why should you have the same rights in all the states?

3. Why should the governor of a state send a criminal back to the state where that person committed a crime?

Section 3

4. Why should people usually not form a new state inside an old one?

5. Explain how West Virginia became a state.

Section 4

6. Why did the colonists want a republican form of government?

ARTICLE V

The Congress, whenever two-thirds of both Houses shall deem it necessary, shall propose amendments to this Constitution, or, on the application of the Legislatures of two-thirds of the several States, shall call a convention for proposing amendments, which, in either case, shall be valid to all intents and purposes, as part of this Constitution, when ratified by the Legislatures of three-fourths of the several States, or by conventions in three-fourths thereof, as the one or the other mode of ratification may be proposed by the Congress; provided that no amendment which may be made prior to the year one thousand eight hundred and eight shall in any manner affect the first and fourth clauses in the Ninth Section of the First Article; and that no State, without its consent, shall be deprived of its equal suffrage in the Senate.

ARTICLE V
HOW TO AMEND THE CONSTITUTION

Whenever two-thirds of both houses think it necessary, Congress may propose changes, or amendments, for the Constitution. Or if two-thirds of the states request it, Congress shall call a convention to propose amendments.

To become a part of the Constitution these proposed amendments must be accepted as follows: They must be approved by three-fourths of the state legislatures. Or three-fourths of the states must call conventions and approve them.

Congress shall say which of these two ways shall be used to approve any particular amendment.

But no amendment before 1808 shall change what we said in Article I, Section 9, about letting slaves come into the states until 1808. No amendment shall change what we said there about putting a direct tax on people. No amendment shall change what we said about every state's having two senators.

All amendments so far have come from Congress, not from the state legislatures.

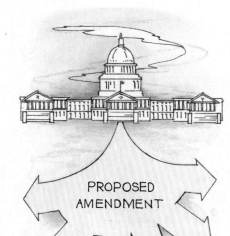

Congress can propose changes to the Constitution. These changes, called amendments, go to the states for approval.

ARTICLE VI

In 1787, we owed more than $75 million in all. The writers of the Constitution put this in to tell the world we were going to pay what we owed.

All debts contracted and engagements entered into before the adoption of this Constitution shall be as valid against the United States under this Constitution as under the Confederation.

We are going to pay what we owed before we wrote this Constitution.

This Constitution and the laws of the United States which shall be made in pursuance thereof and all treaties made, or which shall be made, under the authority of the United States, shall be the supreme law of the land, and the

The Constitution, the laws made by Congress, and our treaties shall be the highest law of our nation.

This means that the Constitution and federal laws rank higher than state laws.

judges in every State shall be bound thereby, anything in the Constitution or laws of any State to the contrary notwithstanding.

All judges shall uphold the Constitution first, no matter what a state law may say.

Every state court judge has to swear to support the Constitution. If a state law goes against the Constitution, it cannot be followed. The Constitution comes first.

The Senators and Representatives before mentioned, and the members of the several State Legislatures, and all executive and judicial officers, both of the United States and of the several States, shall be bound by oath or affirmation to support this Constitution; but no religious

All government and state officers must swear to support this Constitution.

A state officer must swear to uphold the United States Constitution before that officer swears to support the state constitution.

test shall ever be required as a qualification to any office or public trust under the United States.

No government representative shall ever have to take any religious test to get into office.

DISCUSSION: ARTICLES V AND VI

Article V

1. Why were the writers of the Constitution wise in planning a way to make changes in the Constitution?

2. How did they arrange to make people think hard before they changed the Constitution?

Article VI

1. Why should every state court judge swear to support the Constitution?

2. Why did the Constitution writers say that no religious test should ever be used for government offices?

Three days after the Constitution was signed, it was sent to Congress. Congress sent a copy to each state legislature. There were some things in the Constitution that people did not like. There were arguments about the wording, mainly in New York and Virginia. Alexander Hamilton, James Madison, and John Jay wrote the *Federalist* papers to get people to accept the Constitution. The Constitution went into effect before North Carolina and Rhode Island agreed to it. They were waiting for a bill of rights to be added.

Rhode Island did not choose any delegates. Seventy-three men were picked by the states. Fifty-five of them worked at one time or another at the Convention. Forty-two of them were there when the Constitution was signed. Three of these delegates refused to sign.

ARTICLE VII

The ratification of the Conventions of nine States shall be sufficient for the establishment of this Constitution between the States so ratifying the same.

Done in convention by the unanimous consent of the States present the seventeenth day of September in the year of our Lord one thousand seven hundred and eighty-seven, and of the Independence of the United States of America the twelfth.

In witness whereof, we have hereunto subscribed our names.

ARTICLE VII
PUTTING THE CONSTITUTION TO WORK

When nine states hold meetings and agree to this Constitution, the Constitution shall be started in those nine states. (Nine states were two-thirds of the original thirteen states.)

People speaking for all the states here have agreed on this Constitution. It is September 17, 1787. This is the twelfth year our country has been free. We sign our names.

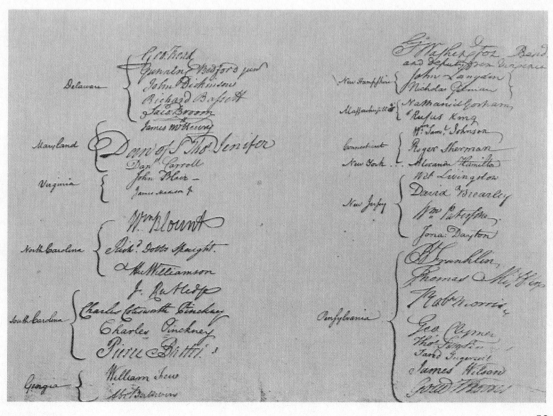

The First Amendment guarantees freedom of religion.

The First Amendment also guarantees freedom of speech and the right to meet peacefully.

THE AMENDMENTS

Some Things to Know	Amendments to the U.S. Constitution	What It Means

The first 10 amendments are the Bill of Rights. They became a part of the Constitution in 1791.

The Supreme Court spends more time on this amendment than on any other.

The writers wanted us to avoid the trouble England had had over religion. England had a "government church," the Church of England. The English people were not free to worship as they wished. Thomas Jefferson said this First Amendment should be a wall between church and state.

AMENDMENT 1

Congress shall make no law respecting an establishment of religion, or prohibiting the free exercise thereof;

or abridging the freedom of speech or of the press;

or the right of the people peaceably to assemble and to petition the Government for a redress of grievances.

AMENDMENT 1
OUR FREEDOM

Congress shall make no law setting up a religion. Congress shall make no law to keep people from following their religion and worshiping as they choose.

Congress shall make no law to keep people from saying what they want or printing what they think.

Congress shall make no law to keep people from meeting peacefully. Congress shall make no law to keep people from asking the government for help when they have not been treated fairly.

The Second Amendment guarantees the right to bear arms.

Police may not break into a person's house without a search warrant.

A capital crime is one for which death is the punishment.

A crime for which death or jail is the punishment.

Grand juries are 12 to 23 persons called in by the county sheriff or the United States district marshall. They must hear witnesses in secret. If they think a person has committed a crime, they send a *true bill* back to the court. If there is not enough evidence to accuse a person of a crime, they write a *no true bill*. Persons charged with a crime by a grand jury must come up for a public trial before another jury.

AMENDMENT 2

A well-regulated militia being necessary to the security of a free State, the right of the people to keep and bear arms shall not be infringed.

AMENDMENT 3

No soldier shall, in time of peace, be quartered in any house without the consent of the owner, nor in time of war, but in a manner to be prescribed by law.

AMENDMENT 4

The right of the people to be secure in their persons, houses, papers, and effects, against unreasonable searches and seizures, shall not be violated, and no warrants shall issue but upon probable cause, supported by oath or affirmation, and particularly describing the place to be searched and the persons or things to be seized.

AMENDMENT 5

No person shall be held to answer for a capital or otherwise infamous crime unless on a presentment or indictment of a grand jury, except in cases arising in the land or naval forces, or in the militia, when in actual service, in time of war or public danger;

AMENDMENT 2
OUR RIGHT TO PROTECT OURSELVES

The people shall have the right to keep guns.

AMENDMENT 3
HOUSING SOLDIERS IN WARTIME

In peace, no soldiers shall live in a person's house unless that person wants them to. In war, a soldier may do so only as the law says.

AMENDMENT 4
PROTECTION FROM SEARCH

People and their houses, papers, and property shall be safe from search. No court shall give a paper, or warrant, to search a person or that person's property except for good reason. Those who want such a search warrant must swear they mean to do right. They must also say just what is to be searched, where the place is, who the people are, and what they are searching for.

AMENDMENT 5
A FAIR TRIAL IN COURT

Nobody has to go to court for a crime that would mean death or jail unless that person is accused by a grand jury.

This will not hold true for army, navy, or militia cases in times of danger to the nation.

This means that no person may be tried twice for the same crime.

This means that no one accused of a crime can be forced to speak against himself or herself.

"Due process" means fairness. The Constitution guarantees that laws passed by Congress have to be fair.

nor shall any person be subject for the same offense to be twice put in jeopardy of life or limb; nor shall be compelled in any criminal case to be a witness against himself, nor be deprived of life, liberty, or property, without due process of law; nor shall private property be taken for public use without just compensation.

People do not have to go to trial a second time if the court freed them the first time. People cannot be made to say anything against themselves in a criminal court. People shall not lose their lives, freedom, or property without being fairly treated, as the Constitution says they should be. The government may not take people's property unless it pays a fair price.

The Fifth Amendment guarantees the right to a prompt, open trial.

AMENDMENT 6

AMENDMENT 6
RIGHTS OF PEOPLE IN COURT

This means that people should not be held in jail a long time before they get their trial.

In all criminal prosecutions, the accused shall enjoy the right to a speedy and public trial, by an impartial jury of the State and district wherein the crime shall have been committed, which district shall have been previously ascertained by law, and to be informed of the nature and cause of the accusation; to be confronted with the witnesses against him; to have compulsory process for obtaining witnesses in his favor, and to have the assistance of counsel for his defense.

People accused of a crime shall have a prompt, open trial. They shall have a fair jury from the state and district where the crime was done.

In some nations, witnesses could write what they wanted to say and never come to court.

In criminal cases, the court gets people a lawyer if they have none themselves. They do not have to pay the lawyer.

The court must tell people why they are being tried. Witnesses against them must speak in front of them. The court shall make witnesses for them come to trial to speak. Accused people shall have a lawyer to defend them.

56

AMENDMENT 7

In suits at common law, where the value in controversy shall exceed twenty dollars, the right of trial by jury shall be preserved, and no fact tried by a jury shall be otherwise re-examined in any court of the United States than according to the rules of the common law.

AMENDMENT 7
JURY TRIALS

In any case about money, the people up for trial may ask for a jury if the amount is over $20. If a jury has ruled on anything, no one can change the ruling unless there is a new trial before another jury or there was a mistake in law made and another court takes the case.

You have a right to be free on bail. *Bail* is money put up to guarantee that a person will show up for trial. The bail may not be out of line with the crime. The writers wanted us to be treated as innocent until *proved* guilty.

AMENDMENT 8

Excessive bail shall not be required,

nor excessive fines imposed,

nor cruel and unusual punishments inflicted.

AMENDMENT 8
PUNISHMENT

People who are to come up for trial shall not have to put up higher bail money than is sensible for the wrong.
Courts shall not ask fines that are out of line with the wrong done.

Courts shall not call for cruel or strange punishment.

Courts in other times often punished by whipping, branding, or cutting off ears. Some people now say that sentencing a person to die for a crime is cruel and unusual punishment.

AMENDMENT 9

The enumeration in the Constitution of certain rights shall not be construed to deny or disparage others retained by the people.

AMENDMENT 9
OTHER RIGHTS

The Constitution gives you certain rights. It cannot list all your rights. If a right is not listed in the Constitution, that does not mean you do not have it.

AMENDMENT 10

The powers not delegated to the United States by the Constitution, nor prohibited by it to the States, are reserved to the States respectively, or to the people.

(End of the Bill of Rights)

AMENDMENT 10
RIGHTS OF STATES

All powers not given to the United States by the Constitution belong to the states or the people.

This part lets states keep their power over such things as marriage and public schools. This amendment was added because most people at that time did not want to give all power to a central government.

This changed Article III, Section 2, of the Constitution.

AMENDMENT 11
(Adopted 1798)

The judicial power of the United States shall not be construed to extend to any suit in law or equity, commenced or prosecuted against one of the United States by citizens of another State, or by citizens or subjects of any foreign state.

AMENDMENT 11
CASES AGAINST STATES

If a person from another state or nation thinks he or she has something against a state, he or she cannot get the case into a United States court.

When voting for a President and a Vice President, the electors used to vote for two candidates. They did not say which one should be President. The candidate who got the most votes became President. The runner-up became Vice President. In 1800, Thomas Jefferson and Aaron Burr got the same number of votes. Then the House of Representatives had to break the tie. They had to vote 36 times before Jefferson finally won. This amendment was written to make it harder for tie votes to happen.

AMENDMENT 12
(Adopted 1804)

The electors shall meet in their respective States and vote by ballot for President and Vice President, one of whom, at least, shall not be an inhabitant of the same State with themselves; they shall name in their ballots the person voted for as President, and in distinct ballots the person voted for as Vice President; and they shall make distinct lists of all persons voted for as President, and of all persons voted for as Vice President, and of the number of votes for each, which lists they shall sign and certify, and transmit, sealed, to the seat of the Government of the United States, directed to the President of the Senate; the President of the Senate shall, in the presence of the Senate and House of Representatives, open all the certificates, and the votes shall then be counted; the person having the greatest number of votes for President shall be the President, if such num-

AMENDMENT 12
A DIFFERENT WAY OF ELECTING THE PRESIDENT AND VICE PRESIDENT

The electors shall meet in their own states. They shall vote for a President and a Vice President. One of these two people shall not be from their own state. The electors shall say which person they want for each office. Then they shall make a list of all the people they have voted for as President. They shall make another list of all the people they have voted for as Vice President. Then they shall write how many votes there are for each person they voted for. They shall sign their names, seal the lists, and send them to the President of the Senate in Washington. The President of the Senate, in front of both houses, shall open the lists. The votes shall be counted. The person having most votes for President shall be President if that person has more than half of all the electoral vote. If no person has over half, the House takes no more than the *three* top people on the list. House members then vote on these three to elect the President. Each state gets only *one* vote no matter how

ALASKA

PRESIDENTIAL
ELECTION
VOTING
BOOTH

REGISTERED MAIL

VOTES

PRESIDENT
OF
SENATE

INAUGURAL

ELECTORS

CITIZENS

HAWAII

Another change is this: If the electoral vote is a tie and House members have to elect the President, they vote for the *three* highest on the list. They used to vote on the *five* highest.

ber be a majority of the whole number of electors appointed; and if no person have such majority, then from the persons having the highest numbers, not exceeding three, on the list of those voted for as President, the House of Representatives shall choose immediately, by ballot, the President. But in choosing the President, the votes shall be taken by States, the representation from each State having one vote; a quorum for this purpose shall consist of a member or members from two-thirds of the States, and a majority of all the States shall be necessary to a

many representatives it has. The vote counts if somebody is voting from two-thirds of the states. To be elected, a person needs votes of more than half of all the states. If the House does not elect a President before the next March 4, the Vice President shall act as President.

59

This date was changed to January 20 in 1933 by the Twentieth Amendment. That amendment says the President's and Vice President's terms shall end at noon on January 20.

The nation went over 60 years without an amendment. Amendments Thirteen, Fourteen, and Fifteen were the Civil War amendments.

Congress had already wiped out slavery in the District of Columbia and the territories. Lincoln's Emancipation Proclamation freed the slaves only in the rebelling Confederate states. Thus, it did not really free those slaves until the Civil War ended. Some people were not sure that Lincoln had the power to free those slaves. Congress passed this amendment to be sure there would be no more slavery.

This means having to work for someone when you do not want to. Congress feared that some slave owners might try to keep their old slaves working. This amendment made sure that former slaves could not be forced to work if they did not want to.

choice. And if the House of Representatives shall not choose a President, whenever the right of choice shall devolve upon them before the fourth day of March next following, then the Vice President shall act as President, as in the case of the death or other constitutional disability of the President. The person having the greatest number of votes as Vice President shall be the Vice President, if such number be a majority of the whole number of electors appointed; and if no person have a majority, then from the two highest numbers on the list, the Senate shall choose the Vice President; a quorum for the purpose shall consist of two-thirds of the whole number of Senators, and a majority of the whole number shall be necessary to a choice. But no person constitutionally ineligible to the office of President shall be eligible to that of Vice President of the United States.

AMENDMENT 13
(Adopted 1865)

Section 1

Neither slavery nor involuntary servitude, except as a punishment for crime whereof the party shall have been duly convicted, shall exist within the United States, or any place subject to their jurisdiction.

The person who has the most votes for Vice President becomes Vice President if that person has over half of all the electoral votes. If no one has over half, the Senate votes for one of the *two* highest on the list. Two-thirds of all the senators must be there to vote to elect a person. The winner must have the votes of more than half of all the senators. If the Constitution keeps a person from running for President, it also keeps that person from running for Vice President.

Abraham Lincoln

AMENDMENT 13
NO SLAVERY

Section 1

People shall not be slaves or have to work for another if they do not want to in any United States land, unless the court punishes them for a crime by making them do work.

60

The Thirteenth Amendment was written to give Black people their freedom. The Fourteenth Amendment was written to make Black people citizens of the United States and of their state. In the Dred Scott case in 1857, the Supreme Court had said that the Constitution writers did not mean a Black person to be a citizen. The Fourteenth Amendment made Black people citizens.

This meant that each state's laws had to be as fair as the federal government's laws. The Fifth Amendment requires the federal government to be fair in its laws. This Fourteenth Amendment requires that the states also be fair.

These are important words. They mean that *all* people must be treated fairly and equally. The Supreme Court has often used these very words to get equal treatment in schools, in jobs, in voting, in housing, and in other things.

Section 2

Congress shall have power to enforce this article by appropriate legislation.

AMENDMENT 14
(Adopted 1868)

Section 1

All persons born or naturalized in the United States, and subject to the jurisdiction thereof, are citizens of the United States and of the State wherein they reside. No State shall make or enforce any law which shall abridge the privileges or immunities of citizens of the United States;

nor shall any State deprive any person of life, liberty, or property without due process of law;

nor deny to any person within its jurisdiction the equal protection of the laws.

Section 2

Congress shall have power to pass laws that will make this amendment work.

AMENDMENT 14
CITIZENS, REPRESENTATIVES, AND DEBTS

Section 1
CITIZENS

All people born in the United States or made citizens of the United States, and who are under the rule of the United States government, are citizens of the United States and of the state in which they live. No state shall make or follow a law that keeps people from getting their rights as United States citizens.

No state shall take people's lives, liberty, or what they own, unless they get fair treatment, as the Constitution says they should.

Anybody under United States rule shall have treatment as fair as anybody else.

The Fourteenth Amendment guarantees every citizen's right to the equal protection of the laws.

Article I, Section 2, of the Constitution counted each slave as only three-fifths of a person. This part of the Fourteenth Amendment changed that. Each Black person was now counted as one person.

Section 2

Representatives shall be apportioned among the several States according to their respective numbers, counting the whole number of persons in each State, excluding Indians not taxed.

This has never been done.

But when the right to vote at any election for the choice of electors for President and Vice President of the United States, Representatives in Congress, the executive and judicial officers of a State, or the members of the Legislature thereof, is denied to any of the male inhabitants of such State, being twenty-one years of age, and citizens of the United States, or in any way abridged, except for participation in rebellion, or other crime, the basis of representation therein shall be reduced in the proportion which the number of such male citizens shall bear to the whole number of male citizens twenty-one years of age in such State.

Section 2
REPRESENTATIVES

The states shall get representatives by the number of people they have. They shall count all people except untaxed Indians.

If a state keeps male citizens from voting in a United States or state election, the number of that state's representatives can be cut down according to the number of people it keeps from voting. The people must be 21 years old, must be male citizens, and must not have done crimes which would keep them from voting.

Section 3

No person shall be a Senator or Representative in Congress, or elector of President and Vice President, or hold any office, civil or military, under the United States, or under any State, who, having previously taken an oath, as a

This had to do with those who fought on the Confederate side in the Civil War.

Section 3
BREAKING OATHS

No person shall hold a government office who once took the oath of office and then became a rebel.

The U.S. government was responsible for paying Union soldiers.

The U.S. government was not responsible for paying Confederate debts.

member of Congress, or as an officer of the United States, or as a member of any State Legislature, or as an executive or judicial officer of any State, to support the Constitution of the United States, shall have engaged in insurrection or rebellion against the same, or given aid or comfort to the enemies thereof. But Congress may, by a vote of two-thirds of each House, remove such disability.

But Congress may clear the person by a two-thirds vote of both houses.

Section 4

The validity of the public debt of the United States, authorized by law, including debts incurred for payment of pensions and bounties for services in suppressing insurrection or rebellion, shall not be questioned. But neither the United States nor any State shall assume or pay any debt or obligation incurred in aid of insurrection or rebellion against the United States, or any claim for the loss or emancipation of any slave; but all such debts, obligations, and claims shall be held illegal and void.

Section 4
DEBTS FROM THE CIVIL WAR

The United States will pay lawful debts, and no one shall question the paying. The United States will pay pensions and other money to Union soldiers for their work in the Civil War. The United States will not pay debts that the Confederate States made in fighting against the United States government. The states must not make such payments either.

Section 5

The Congress shall have power to enforce, by appropriate legislation, the provisions of this article.

Section 5

Congress shall have power to pass laws that will make this amendment work.

63

The Fifteenth Amendment guarantees the voting rights of racial minorities.

AMENDMENT 15
(Adopted 1870)

Section 1

In 1870, this gave Black men the right to vote. It now protects the voting rights of small or minority groups.

The right of citizens of the United States to vote shall not be denied or abridged by the United States or by any State on account of race, color, or previous condition of servitude.

Section 2

The Voting Rights Act of 1965 was enacted under this clause.

The Congress shall have power to enforce this article by appropriate legislation.

AMENDMENT 16
(Adopted 1913)

In 1895, the Supreme Court ruled that Congress could not put a tax on people's income. This amendment gave Congress the right to do so.

The Congress shall have power to lay and collect taxes on incomes, from whatever source derived, without apportionment among the several States, and without regard to any census or enumeration.

AMENDMENT 15
RIGHT TO VOTE

Section 1

No state may keep United States citizens from voting because of their race, their color, or because they were once slaves.

Section 2

Congress shall have power to pass laws that will make this amendment work.

AMENDMENT 16
INCOME TAX

Congress may call for income taxes from all people without trying to get a certain amount from each state.

This amendment changes Article I, Section 3. The state legislatures used to elect the senators. Direct elections by the people make the senators more responsible to them.

The Eighteenth Amendment banned the sale of liquor.

AMENDMENT 17
(Adopted 1913)

The Senate of the United States shall be composed of two Senators from each State, elected by the people thereof for six years; and each Senator shall have one vote. The electors in each State shall have the qualifications requisite for electors of the most numerous branch of the State Legislatures.

When vacancies happen in the representation of any State in the Senate, the Executive Authority of such State shall issue writs of election to fill such vacancies: *Provided,* That the Legislature of any State may empower the Executive thereof to make temporary appointments until the people fill the vacancies by election as the Legislature may direct.

This amendment shall not be so construed as to affect the election or term of any Senator chosen before it becomes valid as part of the Constitution.

AMENDMENT 18
(Adopted 1919)

Section 1

After one year from the ratification of this article the manufacture, sale, or transportation of intoxicating liquors within, the importation thereof into, or the exportation thereof from the United States and all territory subject to the jurisdiction thereof for beverage purposes is hereby prohibited.

AMENDMENT 17
PEOPLE ELECT SENATORS

The Senate shall be made up of two senators from each state. The people shall elect them to 6-year terms. Each senator shall have one vote.

The requirements to vote for Senators shall be the same as those to vote for a legislature representative.

If a senator dies or quits, the governor shall call for an election to elect someone to that office. But the state legislature may tell the governor to choose a person until the people elect a new senator. The legislature shall say how and when the election shall be held.

This amendment shall not change the election or term of a senator chosen before the amendment becomes part of the Constitution.

AMENDMENT 18
LIQUOR

Section 1

This amendment shall be law 1 year after three-fourths of the states pass it: Nobody in the United States lands shall make, sell, or carry liquor that makes a person drunk. Nobody shall send it into the nation. Nobody shall send it out.

65

Section 2

The Congress and the several States shall have concurrent power to enforce this article by appropriate legislation.

Section 2

Congress and the states shall both have power to pass laws needed to make this amendment work.

Section 3

This is the first amendment to have a time limit. Congress wanted to get this amendment question settled within 7 years.

This article shall be inoperative unless it shall have been ratified as an amendment to the Constitution by the Legislatures of the several States, as provided in the Constitution, within seven years from the date of the submission hereof to the States by the Congress.

Section 3

This amendment will not be part of the Constitution unless the state legislatures vote for it as the Constitution says and approve it within 7 years.

Women had been working for the right to vote for years. The work of women in jobs on the home front during World War I helped this amendment pass.
In the 1924 election, only a third of the women who could vote actually cast a ballot. In 1984, 60.8 percent of women who could vote did. The same percentage for men in 1984 was 59 percent.

AMENDMENT 19
(Adopted 1920)

Section 1

The right of citizens of the United States to vote shall not be denied or abridged by the United States or by any State on account of sex.

AMENDMENT 19
WOMEN VOTE

Section 1

No state may keep a citizen from voting because she is a woman.

The Nineteenth Amendment gave women the right to vote.

Section 2

Congress shall have power to enforce this article by appropriate legislation.

AMENDMENT 20
(Adopted 1933)

Section 1

The terms of the President and Vice President shall end at noon on the 20th day of January, and the terms of Senators and Representatives at noon on the 3rd day of January, of the years in which such terms would have ended if this article had not been ratified; and the terms of their successors shall then begin.

Section 2

The Congress shall assemble at least once in every year, and such meeting shall begin at noon on the 3rd day of January, unless they shall by law appoint a different day.

Section 3

If at the time fixed for the beginning of the term of the President, the President-elect shall have died, the Vice President-elect shall become President. If a President shall not have been chosen before the time fixed for the beginning of his term, or if the President-elect shall have failed to

Section 2

Congress shall have power to pass laws that will make this amendment work.

AMENDMENT 20
NEW DATES

Section 1
NEW TERMS OF OFFICE

The President's and Vice President's terms shall end at noon, January 20. Senators' and representatives' terms shall end at noon, January 3. The new officers' terms begin then.

Section 2
MEETINGS OF CONGRESS

Congress shall meet at least once a year. That meeting shall begin at noon, January 3, unless members of Congress pass a law to meet some other day.

Section 3
ACTING PRESIDENT

If the person elected President dies before taking office, the person elected Vice President becomes President. If a President has not been elected when the term should begin, the person elected Vice President shall serve until a person is elected. Congress may make a law saying who shall act as President if neither one is elected. Congress

---

This amendment changes sections of Articles I and II of the Constitution and also the Twelfth Amendment. This ended the 4-month delay between election and the time the winners went into office. Before the change, a lame duck President and Congress stayed in office too long after they were voted out. Now the President and Vice President are sworn in on January 20 instead of on March 4.

This changes Article I, Section 4.

Each year, Congress begins meeting at noon on January 3.

qualify, then the Vice President-elect shall act as President until a President shall have qualified; and the Congress may by law provide for the case where-in neither a President-elect nor a Vice President-elect shall have qualified, declar-ing who shall then act as President, or the manner in which one who is to act shall be selected, and such person shall act accordingly until a President or Vice President shall have qual-ified.

may say how such a person shall be chosen.

Newly elected senators and repre-sentatives move to Washington, DC, to be near their work.

Section 4

The Congress may by law provide for the case of the death of any of the persons from whom the House of Representatives may choose a President whenever the right of choice shall have devolved upon them, and for the case of the death of any of the persons from whom the Senate may choose a Vice President whenever the right of choice shall have devolved upon them.

Section 4

Congress may make laws telling what to do if the House has to elect a President and the person dies. Congress may also make laws telling what to do if the Senate has to elect a Vice Pres-ident and that person dies.

New senators and representatives begin their terms on January 3.

Section 5

Sections 1 and 2 shall take effect on the 15th day of October following the ratification of this article.

Section 5

Sections 1 and 2 shall be law on the October 15 after the states pass this amendment.

Section 6

This article shall be inoperative unless it shall have been ratified as an amendment to the Constitution by the Legislatures of three-fourths of the several States within seven years from the date of its submission.

Section 6

This amendment will not be part of the Constitution unless the state legislatures vote for it as the Constitution says and approve it within 7 years.

AMENDMENT 21
(Adopted 1933)

AMENDMENT 21
REPEAL OF AMENDMENT 18

Section 1

Amendment 18 could not be enforced. Many people felt the government should not tell them what they could drink. Many people broke the law by buying and selling liquor. Much crime resulted. Because it did not work, many people were glad when Amendment 18 was wiped out.

The eighteenth article of amendment to the Constitution of the United States is hereby repealed.

Section 1

The Eighteenth Amendment is out.

Section 2

The transportation or importation into any State, Territory, or possession of the United States for delivery or use therein of intoxicating liquors, in violation of the laws thereof, is hereby prohibited.

Section 2

No one shall break the state liquor laws, though.

Section 3

This article shall be inoperative unless it shall have been ratified as an amendment to the Constitution by conventions in the several

Section 3

This amendment will not be part of the Constitution unless the state meetings vote for it as the Constitution says and approve it within 7 years.

The Constitution writers did not put any limit on the number of terms a President could serve. President George Washington retired after two terms. People thought that made sense. The next 30 Presidents served two terms or less. Then Franklin D. Roosevelt was elected President four times in a row. He died in the first year of his fourth term. After that, it was decided to set a limit of two terms (8 years). This amendment did not apply to President Harry S Truman, who was President at the time. However, after serving almost 8 years, Truman did not run again.

William Harrison had the shortest presidency. He died after serving 1 month of his first term.

Franklin Roosevelt had the longest presidency. He died after serving 3 months of his fourth term.

States, as provided in the Constitution, within seven years from the date of the submission hereof to the States by the Congress

AMENDMENT 22
(Adopted 1951)

Section 1

No person shall be elected to the office of the President more than twice, and no person who has held the office of President, or acted as President, for more than two years of a term to which some other person was elected President shall be elected to the office of the President more than once. But this Article shall not apply to any person holding the office of President when this Article was proposed by the Congress, and shall not prevent any person who may be holding the office of President, or acting as President, during the term within which this Article becomes operative from holding the office of President or acting as President during the remainder of such term.

Section 2

This article shall be inoperative unless it shall have been ratified as an amendment to the Constitution by the Legislatures of three-

AMENDMENT 22
LENGTH OF SERVICE OF PRESIDENT

Section 1

Nobody may be elected President more than twice. Nobody who has been President or acted as President for more than 2 years of somebody else's term shall be elected President more than once. (This means that no one can serve as President for more than 10 years.)

This amendment will not stop the person who is now President from continuing as President. It does not stop the person who will be President when the amendment becomes law from serving as President.

Section 2

This amendment will not be part of the Constitution unless the state legislatures vote for it as the Constitution says and approve it within 7 years.

70

fourths of the several states within seven years from the date of its submission to the States by the Congress.

This amendment gives the people of Washington, DC, the right to vote in presidential elections. They did not have this right until March 29, 1961. The District of Columbia is not a state, but people there do elect one delegate to the House of Representatives.

AMENDMENT 23
(Adopted 1961)

Section 1

The District constituting the seat of Government of the United States shall appoint in such manner as the Congress may direct: A number of electors of President and Vice President equal to the whole number of Senators and Representatives in Congress to which the District would be entitled if it were a State, but in no event more than the least populous State; they shall be in addition to those appointed by the States, but they shall be considered, for the purposes of the election of President and Vice President, to be electors appointed by a State; and they shall meet in the District and perform such duties as provided by the twelfth article of amendment.

Section 2

The Congress shall have power to enforce this article by appropriate legislation.

AMENDMENT 23
WASHINGTON, DC, RESIDENTS GET RIGHT TO VOTE IN PRESIDENTIAL ELECTIONS

Section 1

The District where the United States government is (Washington, DC) shall appoint, in such a way as Congress may say: The number of electors of President and Vice President equal to the number of senators and representatives the District would get if it were a state. The District may not have more electors than the smallest state. The District electors shall vote in presidential elections just as state electors do. They shall meet in the District and do the duties of electors as the Twelfth Amendment says electors should.

Section 2

Congress shall have power to make any laws needed to make this amendment work.

71

AMENDMENT 24
(Adopted 1964)

Section 1

AMENDMENT 24
TAXES AND THE VOTING PRIVILEGE

Section 1

This amendment was put in to make sure that United States citizens would not lose the right to vote in federal elections because they had not paid their taxes. The poll tax had often been used to keep poor people from voting. In 1966, the Supreme Court ruled that the states could not keep citizens from voting in any election—federal, state, or local—because they had not paid a poll tax or any other tax.

The right of citizens of the United States to vote in any primary or other election for President or Vice President, for electors for President or Vice President, or for Senator or Representative in Congress, shall not be denied or abridged by the United States or any State by reason of failure to pay any poll tax or other tax.

No state may keep United States citizens from voting in any primary or general election for President, Vice President, electors for President or Vice President, or for senator or representative in Congress because they have not paid state poll taxes or other taxes.

Section 2

The Congress shall have power to enforce this article by appropriate legislation.

Congress shall have power to make any laws needed to make this amendment work.

AMENDMENT 25
(Adopted 1967)

Section 1

AMENDMENT 25
PRESIDENTIAL SUCCESSION

Section 1

This amendment changes Article II, Section 1, of the Constitution. Before this amendment, there was no way to decide on a Vice President except at a regular election. People were worried about a President's illness. After President John F. Kennedy was killed, and Vice President Lyndon B. Johnson became President, we had no Vice President for almost 14 months.
For a chart showing other times when the United States had no Vice President, see page 76.

In case of the removal of the President from office or of his death or resignation, the Vice President shall become President.

If the President is removed from office, or dies or resigns, the Vice President shall become President.

Section 2

Whenever there is a vacancy in the office of the Vice President, the President shall nominate a Vice President who shall take office upon confirmation by a majority vote of both Houses of Congress.

If there is no Vice President for any reason, the President shall nominate one. If more than half of the Senate and more than half of the House of Representatives vote in favor, that person shall become Vice President.

Section 3

This section makes it possible for the Vice President to do the President's work if the President gets sick. If the President were unable to work and did not resign, our country might be in real trouble. When President Ronald Reagan had his cancer operation in 1985, he turned over his duties to Vice President George Bush for 8 hours.

Whenever the President transmits to the President _pro tempore_ of the Senate and the Speaker of the House of Representatives his written declaration that he is unable to discharge the powers and duties of his office, and until he transmits a written declaration to the contrary, such powers and duties shall be discharged by the Vice President as Acting President.

If the President cannot do the work any longer, the President must say so, in writing, to the leader of the Senate and to the Speaker of the House of Representatives. If the President does so, the Vice President shall become Acting President and do the work. If the President later becomes able to do the work again, the President must again say so in writing.

Section 4

If the Vice President and most of the Cabinet think the President is too sick to do the job, they tell the Senate and the House. The Vice President can then become Acting President until the President gets well. If the President says he is ready and the Vice President and Cabinet agree, the President goes back on the job. If the Vice President and Cabinet do not agree, the Congress will say who is right.

Whenever the Vice President and a majority of the principal officers of the executive departments, or such other body as Congress may by law provide, transmit to the President _pro tempore_ of the Senate and the Speaker of the House of Representatives their written declaration that the President is unable to discharge the powers and duties of his office, the Vice President shall immediately assume the powers and duties of the office of Acting President.

Thereafter, when the President transmits to the President _pro tempore_ of the Senate and the Speaker of the House of Representatives his written declaration that no inability exists, he shall resume the powers

If the Vice President and more than half of the Cabinet (or any other group that Congress sets up by law) think that the President can no longer do the work, they should say so in writing. They must send their written statement to both the leader of the Senate and the Speaker of the House. If they do, the Vice President immediately becomes Acting President and does the work.

If, later, the President is ready again to do the work, the President must say so in writing. The President must send the statement to both the leader of the Senate and the Speaker of the House. When the President has done so, the President again does

73

In 1919, halfway through his second term as President, Woodrow Wilson had a stroke. For the rest of his time in office, he had to rely heavily on the help of his wife, Edith.

Vice President Bush was legally Acting President while President Reagan underwent surgery.

Under the Constitution, the states set the age at which people could vote. Most states said age 21. Two states went as low as age 18. This amendment gives all

and duties of his office unless the Vice President and a majority of the principal officers of the executive departments, or such other body as Congress may by law provide, transmit within four days to the President *pro tempore* of the Senate and the Speaker of the House of Representatives their written declaration that the President is unable to discharge the powers and duties of his office. Thereupon Congress shall decide the issue, assembling within forty-eight hours for that purpose if not in session. If the Congress, within twenty-one days after the receipt of the latter written declaration, or, if Congress is not in session, within twenty-one days after Congress is required to assemble, determines by two-thirds vote of both Houses that the President is unable to discharge the powers and duties of his office, the Vice President shall continue to discharge the same as Acting President; otherwise, the President shall resume the powers and duties of his office.

AMENDMENT 26
(Adopted 1971)

Section 1

The right of citizens of the United States, who are eighteen years of age or older, to vote shall not be denied or abridged by the

the work. But if the Vice President and more than half of the Cabinet (or any other group that Congress sets up by law) do not think the President is able to do the work, they must say so in writing. Within 4 days they must send such a written statement to both the leader of the Senate and the Speaker of the House. If they do, Congress must decide within 21 days if the President is or is not able to do the work. If Congress is not having meetings at the time, the members must meet within 48 hours. Then Congress has 21 days to make a decision. If two-thirds of the Senate and two-thirds of the House vote that the President is not able to work, the Vice President stays as Acting President and does the work. If two-thirds of the Senate and two-thirds of the House do not so vote, the President again does the work.

AMENDMENT 26
THE VOTE FOR 18-YEAR-OLDS

Section 1

Any person who will be 18 years of age by election day should be allowed to register and vote in all elections—national, state, and local.

74

The Twenty-sixth Amendment gave 18-year-olds the right to vote.

persons 18 or older the right to vote in all elections. Congress hoped this amendment would cause more young people to get interested in our government. But only about one out of three of those aged 18, 19, and 20 voted for President in 1984.

United States or any State on account of age.

Section 2

The Congress shall have the power to enforce this article by appropriate legislation.

Section 2

Congress shall have the power to pass laws that will make this amendment work.

President	No Vice President	Reason
James Madison	April 1812–March 1813 Nov. 1814–March 1817	George Clinton and Elbridge Gerry died in office.
Andrew Jackson	Dec. 1832–March 1833	John C. Calhoun resigned after being elected to the Senate.
John Tyler	1841–1845	Tyler succeeded William Henry Harrison, who died.
Millard Fillmore	1850–1853	Fillmore succeeded Zachary Taylor, who died.
Franklin Pierce	April 1853–March 1857	William R. D. King died shortly after taking office.
Andrew Johnson	1865–1869	Johnson succeeded Abraham Lincoln, who was assassinated.
Ulysses S. Grant	Nov. 1875–March 1877	Henry Wilson died in office.
Chester A. Arthur	1881–1885	Arthur succeeded James A. Garfield, who was assassinated.
Grover Cleveland	Nov. 1885–March 1889	Thomas A. Hendricks died after 8 months in office.
William McKinley	Nov. 1889–March 1901	Garret A. Hobart died in office.
Theodore Roosevelt	Sept. 1901–March 1905	Theodore Roosevelt succeeded William McKinley, who was assassinated.
William H. Taft	Oct. 1912–March 1913	James S. Sherman died in office.
Calvin Coolidge	1923–1925	Coolidge succeeded Warren G. Harding, who died.
Harry S Truman	1945–1949	Truman succeeded Franklin D. Roosevelt, who died.
Lyndon B. Johnson	Nov. 1963–1965	Johnson succeeded John F. Kennedy, who was assassinated.
Richard M. Nixon	Oct. 10, 1973–Dec. 6, 1973	Spiro T. Agnew resigned after being charged with wrongdoing.
Gerald R. Ford	Aug. 9, 1974–Dec. 19, 1974	Ford succeeded Richard M. Nixon, who resigned under threat of impeachment.

WHAT THE CONSTITUTION MEANS TO YOU

This Constitution belongs to you. As an American, you are part owner of this Constitution of the United States of America. It guarantees to you the freedoms and privileges that many people in other lands do not have. It spells out the rules to make sure that Americans will be governed justly and fairly.

Remember that . . .

1. You and your fellow Americans know exactly what your Constitutional rights are. You know how you will be governed. You have these rights and rules set down in print in our Constitution. People in many other lands do not have such statements. Their rulers often make their own laws. These rulers may be cruel and unjust to their people.

2. Our Constitution need never get out of date as times change. It wisely spells out how to change our rules when necessary. Three-fourths of our states have to agree before we can change the rules. The changes, or amendments, must have much support before we add them to the Constitution. We have to take time to think about them first. People in other lands often have to rebel against their rulers when they want changes in their governments. They often see no other way to get the changes that they need and want.

3. Our Constitution gives you the right to vote. If you are 18 years old or older, you may vote for any leader or representative you like. We often have many candidates to choose from. We have more than one political party. We have a chance to elect the very best persons to represent us. In Communist nations, only one political party is allowed. A small group of leaders decides who will run the nation. The people do not have a choice of leaders when they vote.

4. Our Constitution lets you be free to speak your mind. In our democracy, people can say what they think. We can talk openly about politics. We may say that our President is wrong about something. We may say that Congress is wrong. Our government cannot stop us from speaking freely. We believe we should tell our leaders when we think they are wrong. We also have the freedom to get our friends to support what we think and say. In many nations, people do not have these freedoms. They do not dare speak out against their rulers. They are afraid to say what they really think.

5. Our Constitution says you may worship—or not worship—as you please. You may go to any church you want to—or not go at all. We Americans have many different churches. The Constitution forbids anybody from making us belong to a particular church. We are free to believe what we want to believe. In Communist nations, the rulers would rather not have churches. They let their people know that they want to get rid of all religion. Many of their people are afraid to say that they believe in God.

6. Our Constitution keeps our newspapers, magazines, and books and our radio and TV stations free. They can give us information about what is going on. They tell us what is happening in the White House and in Congress. They tell us what our leaders are doing and saying in the state capitals. They tell us what our mayors and city council members are doing. Because we are informed, we can vote sensibly. In fact, we can run for office ourselves. In some nations, the newspapers print only what the rulers want printed. The people are not allowed to read other papers. They may not listen to radio broadcasts from other lands. The leaders will not let the people see or hear anything against the government.

7. Our Constitution gives you freedom to travel as you wish. You can cross state lines without being stopped. You can go to Maine or Florida or California. You can fly or sail to Alaska or Hawaii. You can get a passport and go to Africa or Asia or Europe or Australia. You can take a job there if you want to. The leaders of some nations do not give their people such freedom to travel. The Communist leaders of East Germany built a great 29-mile wall in Berlin in 1961 to keep East Germans from escaping into West Germany. Their guards have shot and killed people who have tried to flee from East Germany to freedom in the West.

8. Our Constitution gives you freedom to choose your schools. Your family could have sent you to a public school, a church school, or a private school. You may apply to any trade school, college, or university. You may go as far in school as you wish. Any American who can do the work can go through high school and college. Some other nations do not give their people this freedom. Some test all students when they are in the fourth grade. Those who score well may go to schools that prepare them for the universities. When they graduate, they go to the universities to become dentists, doctors, and lawyers. The other fourth graders are shut off from the preparatory schools and universities. They are sent to vocational schools to learn a trade. In some nations, education is directed by the government to suit the rulers' needs.

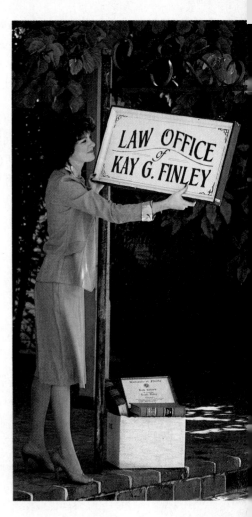

9. Our Constitution gives you freedom to choose the kind of work you do. You can be a mechanic, a doctor, a lawyer, a carpenter, a business manager, a professor, a secretary, or a member of the clergy. You can start your own business and be your own boss. You can run for office. If you have the skills, you can make money as a professional athlete. Many other nations do not give their people such freedom. In some nations, the government tells you what your job will be. The government tells you how much you will earn.

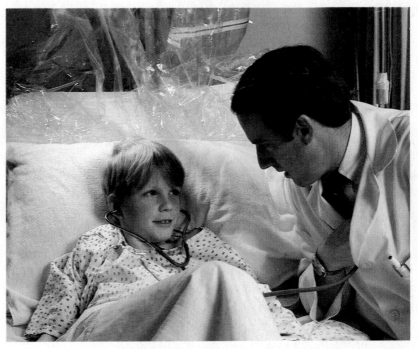

10. Our Constitution protects you by means of just laws and fair treatment in court. If you are accused of a crime, you are considered innocent until proved guilty. If you cannot afford a lawyer, you get one free to defend you. You get a fair trial in court. You get a jury of your fellow citizens. You have a right to make your accuser face you. If you are found guilty, you will get no cruel and unusual punishment. In some nations, you can get a long jail sentence before your trial even starts. Some governments throw people into jail without giving reasons. Some punish people for what they write and say. Some can and do mistreat and torture prisoners. The United States opposes such violations of human rights. Our Constitution makes our nation a symbol of freedom to people around the world.

84

CONSTITUTION VOCABULARY

abolish. Do away with.

abridge. Shorten; cut down. To *abridge* people's rights means to take some of them away, to keep people from some of their rights.

adjourn. To hold up business for a while; to stop a meeting for a while. When Congress *adjourns,* the members hold up business until the next time they meet.

admiralty. People who head a navy; a court in which navy cases are settled. The Supreme Court takes *admiralty* cases—that is, court cases about ships.

affirmation. Saying that something is true. Some people believe it is wrong to take an oath—to swear that something is true. Such people may make an *affirmation* instead of an oath. If a person *affirms* a lie in court, he or she is guilty of perjury.

alliance. A union; an agreement between nations to support each other. For example: "England and France formed an *alliance.*"

ambassador. An official representative of one government sent to another nation to deal with the government there. The official usually lives in the other nation and there represents his or her government.

amendment. A change. An *amendment* to the Constitution is a change in the Constitution.

appellate. Having anything to do with an appeal, or call for help. If people feel they did not get fair treatment in a lower court, they *appeal* to a higher court. Courts for appeals are called *appellate* (uh PEL it) courts.

apportion. To give out parts, or portions. "Representatives shall be *apportioned* among the States" means the different states will get their fair share of representatives.

appropriate. Fit, right, proper—when it is used as an adjective. To give *appropriate* (uh PROH pree it) punishment means to give the right or proper punishment. *Appropriate* (uh PROH pree AYT) means to take or to set apart when used as a verb. To *appropriate* money for the army means to set aside money for the army.

appropriation. The thing that is set aside for someone, especially money. So we say, "The *appropriation* (uh PROH pree AY shun) of Congress for the army was not enough."

approve. To OK; to agree to; to like a thing. "The President *approved* the bill" means the President liked the bill and agreed to it.

arsenal. A place where you make or store guns or other army equipment.

attaint. To prove guilty. Usually it means also to take away a person's rights given by the government. A person who is *attainted* might not be able to vote. See **bills of attainder.**

bail. Money or other security put up to guarantee that an accused person will show up at the trial.

ballot. A printed or written strip of paper for voting, or the voting. In many places, voting machines have taken the place of paper ballots.

bankruptcy. If people cannot pay what they owe, they may say so to the courts. They say they are bankrupt. The court then picks a person who is called a *trustee* to settle the people's affairs. The trustee takes what the people own and tries to raise as much as she or he can to pay what the people owe.

bill. A proposed law given to a lawmaking body for passage.

bills of attainder. See Column 1, Article I, Section 9.

breach of peace. Breaking the peace; disturbing the safety or peace of people, as by causing a riot.

Cabinet. The heads of the President's executive departments. The Cabinet includes the secretaries of agriculture; commerce; defense; education; energy; health and human services; housing and urban development; interior; labor; state; transportation; and the treasury; plus the attorney general.

capital. As in *capital* crime. Means any crime for which death is the punishment.

capitation. From a word meaning "head." *Capitation* is a tax laid on people by counting them—that is, counting heads. This means the same tax on all people instead of a tax on what people own. A poll tax is capitation.

census. A count of the people.

certificate. A paper, or document, that says something is true. It serves as a witness. When the electors send in their lists, they *certify* the list, or say it is true. The list is then a certificate.

Chief Justice. The judge who presides over or acts as president of the Supreme Court.

civil. Anything to do with a citizen. *Civil* cases in court are cases about a person's rights as a citizen. Civil cases have nothing to do with crime.

Civil Rights Act of 1964. The strongest civil rights bill in American history. It ordered restaurants, hotels, and other businesses to serve people of all races, colors, and religions. It barred unequal treatment by employers and unions. It also provided for a cutting off of federal money from programs that did not treat everybody fairly.

common law. The general law of a nation or community.

compact. An agreement or treaty. To make a *compact* between states means to make an agreement between states.

compensation. Pay.

compulsory. Forced. *Compulsory* training means training you have to take.

concur. To agree. "The President may make treaties if two-thirds of the Senate *concurs,* or agrees."

concurrence. An agreement. *Concurrence* of Congress means agreement of Congress with someone.

concurrent. Running together; happening at the same time. If Congress and the states have *concurrent* power, they both have power at the same time.

Confederate States. The 11 Southern states that withdrew from the United States during 1860 and 1861: South Carolina, Mississippi, Florida, Alabama, Georgia, Louisiana, Texas, Virginia, Arkansas, Tennessee, North Carolina.

confederation. A joining together; a union. The Southern states formed a *confederation* in 1860.

Congressional Record. A printed record of what is said and done in Congress each day. Members of Congress may put in other information besides what they say in their speeches. Such a record has been printed under different names since 1799. The present *Record* began in 1873.

construe. To explain or to interpret. To *construe* a rule means to figure out what the rule means, to interpret it.

consul. A representative of a nation who lives in another nation. A consul's work is to protect his or her fellow citizens and their property in that foreign nation; the consul also acts as their law adviser.

controversy. A dispute; a debate; an argument.

convene. To meet; especially to meet as a special group.

convention. A meeting.

conviction. Being found guilty. If you are *convicted* of a crime, the court says you are guilty of the crime. Used another way, it also means something you believe: "I have the *conviction* that that person is wrong."

corruption (of blood). Used to mean spoiled, bad, tainted. When a person is guilty of treason, the Constitution says there shall be no *"corruption* of blood." That means the children of the guilty person shall not suffer because of what the parent did.

court of appeals. One of 11 federal courts that rank above district courts. When federal cases are appealed, they go from district courts to a court of appeals. Some states also have courts of appeals.

Declaration of Independence. The statement of the Second Continental Congress, passed on July 4, 1776, saying that the 13 American colonies were free of British rule. It was written mainly by Thomas Jefferson for a committee that included Benjamin Franklin, John Adams, Roger Sherman, and R. R. Livingston. It is preserved in Washington, DC.

deem. To think; to suppose. To *deem* a law right is to think it is right.

deprive. To take away from. To *deprive* citizens of their rights is to take rights away from them.

devolve. To roll down; to pass from one to another; to be handed down. If a duty *devolves* on you, it comes down to you; it is given to you.

diminished. Made less.

disapprove. To vote against. If Congress *disapproves* a bill, they vote against it, they turn it down.

district. A part of some land. A state is divided into *districts,* or parts.

district court. Any of 94 federal courts in which cases are first heard.

domestic. Having to do with home. *Domestic* trade means trade at home, or in our own nation.

domestic tranquility. Peace at home.

due process. Complete and fair working of the law. See Amendment 6.

duties. Used in the Constitution to mean a tax on goods coming into a nation.

elector. One who elects. In the Constitution, usually the persons elected by the voters to vote for President and Vice President. Together the electors form the electoral college.

eligible. Fit or qualified. If you are *eligible* for a job, you are fit for it; you have qualifications for it.

emancipation. Setting free. Lincoln *emancipated* the slaves—that is, he set them free.

Emancipation Proclamation. A statement issued by President Abraham Lincoln on January 1, 1863. It said that all slaves in the Confederate States were free.

emolument. Pay; gain; profit. If people receive an *emolument,* they receive pay or reward for what they have done.

enumeration. A numbering or naming; a counting. *Enumeration* of people is counting them—taking a census.

equal rights amendment. The proposed 27th amendment to the Constitution, known as the ERA. It stated: "Equality of rights under the law shall not be denied or abridged by the United States or by any State on account of sex." Congress passed the ERA in 1972. Only 35 of the necessary 38 states (three-fourths of the 50 states) had ratified the ERA by March 22, 1979, the end of the 7-year period allowed to ratify. It was therefore not added to the Constitution.

equity. Being just; fairness. A court of *equity* is a court of justice.

excise. A tax for making, selling, or using goods inside a nation.

executing. Doing. If the House and Senate are *executing* their duties, they are doing them.

executive. The branch of our government that puts our laws into action. Also, the person who manages, or directs. The chief *executive* is the President.

executive authority. Authority is the right to do a thing. *Executive authority* is the right to do something, but this authority is given only to the President.

expedient. Used as "proper" or "wise" in the Constitution. "It is *expedient* that Congress make a new law." That is, it is wise; it will help us if Congress makes a new law.

expel. To drive out; to force out.

expenditure. What you spend.

expire. Die out.

export. To sell goods to another nation; something sent *out of* a nation. We *export* goods to Europe (verb). Some of our *exports* go to Europe (noun).

ex post facto. See explanation in Article 1, Section 9.

federal. Anything to do with a central government that is over a number of states.

Federalist. A member of an American political party that favored a strong central government.

felony. A serious crime.

forfeiture. The loss of your right to something because you have not done your part. You may *forfeit* your rights to citizenship by doing treason.

grant. A gift, especially from a government. A state *grant* of lands is a gift of lands from the state.

grievance. A complaint. If you have a *grievance,* you feel you have not had fair treatment.

habeas corpus. See explanation in Article I, Section 9.

illegal. Against the law.

immunity. Freedom from. *Immunity* from arrest means being free from arrest. For example, members of Congress have some immunity from arrest while they are meeting.

impeach. To accuse a government officer of doing wrong. See explanation in Article I, Section 2.

import. To buy goods from another nation; something brought *into* a nation. We *import* goods from Asia (verb). Some of our *imports* come from Asia (noun).

impost. A tax on goods.

indictment. Accusing somebody before a court or charging somebody with a crime by a grand jury. If members of a grand jury think people have done a wrong, they bring the people into court, or *indict* them.

inferior. Lower. The Supreme Court is the highest court in the nation. Other courts are lower, or *inferior,* courts.

infringe. To take part of. If a person *infringes* on your rights, that person is taking part of your rights.

inoperative. Not operating; not working. If a law is *inoperative,* it is dead, not working.

insurrection. A rebellion; a civil war; fighting against the government.

invasion. Going into a nation to take it over.

involuntary servitude. Working against your will; being a slave.

jeopardy. Danger.

journal. In the Constitution, a record of what is done. Each house keeps a *journal,* or record, of what it has done.

judicial. Having to do with judging. The *judicial* branch of government is the judging branch—it includes the courts and judges.

judicial review. The power of courts to say whether lawmakers have made proper laws. See Article III, Section 2.

junction. A joining together.

jurisdiction. The right to rule. If a court has *jurisdiction,* it has the right to rule. State courts would not have jurisdiction over United States government cases.

lame duck. An officeholder who has failed to be reelected but whose term is not yet over.

legislative. Having to do with laws or lawmaking. Congress is the *legislative* branch of government because it legislates, or makes laws.

legislature. The people who have the job of making laws. In the Constitution, it usually means the senators and representatives of a state.

letters of marque. See explanation in Article I, Section 8.

letters of reprisal. Same as **letters of marque.** See explanation in Article I, Section 8.

levy. To raise; to collect. To *levy* taxes means to collect taxes.

magazine. A place where goods are stored, especially ammunition.

maritime. Anything to do with the ocean or sea.

migration. Movement of people from one place to another, especially a move from one nation or climate to another.

militia. State soldiers. They are called out to help in time of danger.

minister. A representative of one nation who deals with another nation's government.

misdemeanor. A small wrongdoing. A *misdemeanor* is not as bad as a felony.

National Guard. A U.S. Army and Air Force organization in each state and in the District of Columbia. Guardsmen enlist and attend weekly training periods all year. The President may order National Guard groups into service during a national emergency. State governors may use them during strikes, riots, and disasters.

naturalize. In the Constitution, to give the rights of a citizen born in our nation to a person born in another nation.

nobility. Persons forming the noble class in a nation, such as dukes, earls, barons, and the like.

nominate. To name; to name for an office. "I *nominate* Mr. Smith as president."

Parliament. The British lawmaking body.

petition. As a noun, a plea or an appeal. As a verb, to beg for. The people may *petition* Congress for help.

preamble. An opening statement that explains the reasons for writing a law or a constitution.

prescribe. To direct; to give directions; to order.

prior. Before; earlier.

proceedings. Things which are done, usually in meetings.

prohibit. To stop; to hinder; to forbid. Congress may *prohibit* a state from doing certain things.

propose. To suggest; to offer a plan. Congress may *propose* a new law.

prosecution. The pressing of a case against someone in court.

pro tempore. For the time being; for a while. A president *pro tempore* is president for only a while.

quarter. In the Constitution, a verb meaning to house soldiers. "The army found homes in which to *quarter* the troops."

quorum. The number of members you need to be able to go ahead and do business. Usually a *quorum* is more than half the members.

ratify. To OK something; to approve. The states must *ratify*, or approve, amendments.

redress. Setting a thing right. If the people ask Congress for "*redress* of wrong," they ask it to see that a wrong be made right.

regulations. Rules.

repeal. To call back. If Congress *repeals* a law, it calls it back, takes it off the books, ends it.

representative. One who represents. A *representative* is chosen to speak or act for a group.

reprieve. If the President gives a *reprieve* to a condemned person, the President holds off, or delays, that person's death.

republican form of government. A government in which the voters have ruling power through the representatives they elect. See Article IV, Section 5.

resident. One who resides, or lives, somewhere. Thus, a *resident* of a state is one who lives in a state.

resolution. Something said by vote of a group. If Congress makes a *resolution* to raise taxes, the members, as a body, say they are going to raise taxes.

revenue. Money coming in.

seizure. Grabbing someone or something by force. *Seizure* of citizens usually means arresting them.

session. A meeting.

Speaker (of the House). The House of Representatives elects its own leader, who conducts its meetings. The leader is called *Speaker* of the House.

suffrage. In the Constitution, the right to vote in politics.

suspend. To hold up for a while. If Congress *suspends* the paying of a tax, Congress stops it or holds it up.

tender. To give, or something you give. You may *tender,* or give, your resignation. We also say that our money is "legal *tender.*" That is, we can give it lawfully to pay for something.

territory. An area that belongs to a nation but is not part of that nation. Before new states were brought into the Union, they were often called *territories*.

tonnage. How much in tons a ship carries. To tax *tonnage* means to tax ships by the load of goods they carry.

treason. Fighting or working against your own nation or your nation's government.

treaty. An agreement, usually between different nations after a war. Enemy nations usually sign peace *treaties*.

tribunal. A court. Lower *tribunals* are courts lower than the Supreme Court.

true bill. A statement from a grand jury saying that an accused person should be brought to trial in court. See Amendment 5.

unanimous. All voting the same way. A *unanimous* vote means all voters vote the same.

uniform. The same. "*Uniform* taxes" means the same taxes for everybody.

valid. Right; truthful. A *valid* argument is a truthful, or right, argument. Something may be valid legally; that is, it is right according to law.

vest. To give a right or power to someone. The Constitution *vests* the President with the veto.

veto. The power to stop or to say no to something in government. The President may *veto* a bill from Congress; that is, turn it down, say no to it.

Voting Rights Act of 1965. A law that ended the use of reading tests to qualify a person to vote.

warrant. A paper, or an order, from a court judge that says people may be arrested or their houses may be searched.

writ. An order, in the name of a court or of the government, saying that something shall be done.